The Sovereignty of God's Silence

He that hath an ear,

let him hear what the spirit, sayeth to the churches.

Revelation 3:6

William Thompson Jr

Copyright 2023

By: William Thompson Jr

Published By

Write Everlasting Tips,

Publishing Company

Printed in the United States of America

ISBN 9-9755994-5-3
ISBN 978-0975599457

To contact author write

Write Everlasting Tips Publishing Co.

P. O. Box 10854

Fort Worth, Texas 76114-0854

Unless otherwise indicated, all scripture quotations are from the KJV,,

All rights reserved, Written permission must be secured from the publisher to use or reproduce any part of this book, except for brief quotations embodied in church related publications, critical review or articles.

Dedication

To all who have already, and to all who will eventually tune in to the frequency of God's voice through His Written word; you are so Loved and cared for!

As God has not excluded you from the divine plan of His Eternal Intention for all of humanity, I have accepted the task to pen this work of definitive clarity to aid any reader to refine the search for God through His written word, and through prayer.

Beloved of God, in these times of which we are now living, through it all, Listen For His Love!

God Loves You Out Loud!

To my family ~ Phyllis Lynette Thompson
Joseph E & Renee, Taylor;
Misty M., Jilysia L., Aaron L., William III.......
Love You All
Mother Daisy Thompson
Mother Lula M. Richard

Table of Contents

Dedication..........................III

About The Author..................IV

Introduction.........................IX

Chapter 1. Generation of Too Much Noise.........19

Chapter 2. What Silences Him.......................31

Chapter 3. God's Word Spoken And Written.....45

Chapter 4. Discerning God's Silence..................55

Chapter 5. Unrestricted Lord...........................67

Chapter 6. God; Treads Above Sound................79

Chapter 7. Disdained God's Order....................91

Chapter 8. He Has Already Spoken..................103

Chapter 9. Right Where He Is.......................115

Chapter 10. Jesus Christ; Silence....................125

Conclusion............................137

About The Author

William Thompson Jr

Born March 12, 1961 in El' Paso, Texas, to the union of the late Rev. William Thompson Sr. & Rev. Daisy Y. Mclawler-Thompson; the family later relocated to Fort Worth, Texas in 1967 where he grew up in the church singing in the choir, learning to study his own bible, and participating in all of the youth activities faithfully.

He has been a partaker in several activities and auxiliaries. Most of all he is a servant to the body of Christ. An avid worker and a giver to the church unselfishly. He thoroughly operates impeccable as an anointed Prophet of God; whereas he has ministered to many people in the Kingdom of God across the country, and over the phone in India, Africa, and London. He is known and respected as a "True Prophet" of God.

He has been ministering the gospel since Feb. 7,1982, and has engaged in studies and training of the bible. He has been in the church all of his natural life and has the experience of a faithful churchman which lends the passion for which he ministers the gospel of God. He has been ordained since June 1998.

By the age of 3 years he had already began to express a passion to play the piano and to preach the Gospel. He is a talented instrumentalist, and has composed many songs. He has ministered in music for ministries in the DFW Metro-plex, and OKC, OK. He has traveled with evangelist, and has been the guest musician for many revivals, musicals, weddings, conferences, recordings and etc.

His uncle; the Late Apostle Russell Thompson, laid his hand on him at the age of 11, from that point on he knew that there was more for him in the Lord. He moved to the next level of worship in an effort to get to that which he desired most of the Lord.

Pastor Thompson has crossed the lines of denominational affiliations as a friend and brother, enabling him to be identified as a child of God and not Just a Baptist, a Methodist, a Pentecostal, or for that matter, just another member of the Church Of God In Christ!

He founded and pastored the Tried Whole Truth Foundation Ministry; in Fort Worth, Texas; As instructed by the Lord he later changed the name to The Spoken Word Center where he had 8 [1998-2005] years of successful ministry under both the names.

Souls were indeed saved, people were filled with

the Holy Ghost; we observed miracles of healing and deliverance; demons cast out; lives changed and many ministries were realized and answered to the call of God.

He founded and established the Spoken Word Center, School of Prophetic Excellence 2003. As of late as we are re-launching the ministry, we have again changed the name of the ministry to The Kingdom Impact Center of the Spoken Word Church, Int.

We have been instrumental in working with and for several different ministries since as of late 2005 until 2020. We have been commissioned to go on forward full force with the ministry of the Kingdom Impact Center of the Spoken Word Church.

He has since preached many revivals where deliverance and the manifested presence of the Lord are witnessed. He has become an avid teacher to those who are new to the body of Christ, instructing them to know and to practice the presence of God in pure worship and praise to our God; in Christ Jesus.

He is a real true lover of people; especially to those who are of the household of faith across the board; if you can love him, and even if you can't, he's committed to loving you.

His endeavor is to serve the people of the Lord everywhere that will receive of the awesome gift of the Holy Ghost to which he has been endowed.

Introduction

The Sovereignty of God's Silence

Bless you all in the very present and glorious name of our *"Sovereign Lord; The Savior, "Jesus Christ"*. The most powerfully unmatched deity of all of Heaven and Earth. Many people are knowledgeable of what He's done, but they don't really know who He Is! The greater damaging issues of the people of the churches is that there is not enough knowledge accepted of the *"Lord."*

We are excited and blown away, as the scripture informs us that "Jesus" walked on the sea, and calmed the howling blast of the wind. And commanded the elevated angry waves to be seated and to rest at the designated sea level, with just one sentence, (three words) *"peace be still!"*

However, not many people who read the scripture are truly convinced that *"Jesus"* is the creator and the maker of the water that He is now walking on. This same Jesus walks over the earth, never weary of the journey. He's always seeing us with His eyes, Protecting us with the *"word of His mouth"*.

Before darkness can ever fall on us, or over our lives, He has already seen us and ascribe the right remedy and answer to our need, through answer to our prayers. The Lord has contiguously spoken over us already fitting the needs of our prayers, but we must be attuned to Him, and ready to receive from Him.

You do know that it is this same "LORD AND SAVIOR", that we who are surrendered to His saving sacrifice at the "CROSS OF CALVARY, ON GOLGOTHA'S HILL", that we look to and always expect to be shielded from all hurt harm and danger. NO Matter What!

It is a great privilege, and undeserved honor and so much more than that; to be kept by the savior in these dark times in which we are now living. But, it is also by reason of His great Love for us all, that He keeps us. It's been no accident or mere incidental happenstance, that God has involved His great and mighty powerful hand into our daily affairs.

He's always intended to be here for us all, knowing that we could never on our own, navigate to chart our own path to make it through our journey in this world. God's never had His back turned away from humanity, knowing that we are His most prized creation in the earth. According to the influence of Satan, man sinned, falling under the deception of the satanic scheme in the Garden.

As result of the previously mentioned details in the story of our beginning here in the earth, our true story has been multi faceted to bespeak of so much more than only of our creation, as human beings.

Reading through the word of God, the bible itself reveals the fatal struggle of Satan to unleash an hostile take over in the nature of mankind. He was still yet desiring to be like the most high God.

Amazingly, Satan who desired to be even greater and higher than the most high God, could not even start from within himself to create anything, simply because he is also a created being. Where to start would forever be his plight. God simply said it and it was so; Satan said it and it has never been so! As simple as that!

God simply exists because God Is all powerfully self exis-

Introduction

tent! From the beginning Satan was on the lesser side of the creating process. Rebelling against God eventually put him on the forever losing side of creation. So much more was begun in the existence of all mankind at the beginning process of us living here on the earth.

According to the book of Genesis in the Holy Bible, we first witnessed the separating account of man and of God who created man. Whereas, the divine fellowship was severed and thought to be depleted forever, as God is an eternal God. It was possibly Satan's idea indeed for man to have been left here all alone, without God, to make it all by themselves.

Entering this reading journey, we will travel through the sovereign portal of God's speaking authority in all of Heaven and in all the Earth. *"GOD SAID!"* And it is even so to this very day in which we are living right now. We understand that nothing that *"GOD"* has ever said could be *"UN-SAID"*.

The greater struggles of humanity nowadays, are all along the boundary lines of what *"GOD"* has already said! About the affairs and the living requirements of mankind all over the earth, it is already written! The fact that so many of us adhere to the *"WORD OF GOD"*, because we accept it, as well as obey *"THE WRITTEN WORD OF GOD"*, creates a grave since of discomfort for so many.

"GOD'S WORD" does not establish platforms to accept sin, or the sinful behavior of man according to the lawful regulations of man's desired behavior in the earth. Unfortunately, the bible is not like unto the Berlin Wall, man can't take tools and machinery and tear it down. Neither can it ever be destroyed. *PSALMS 119:89*

The adamantly sinful people of the earth and even of the world, are often quoted as saying to the people of *"GOD"* who are advocates of the lawful mandates of faith and of righteousness, according to the word of God. *"Show it to me in*

The Sovereignty of God's Silence

the bible that it's wrong!"

Although most of them, on an average, are not even open to reading the bible. They have never believed the bible to even be true!

Many have embraced the idealism of the scripture, which suggests to them, to just look away. People from many generations prior to the present generation, have never had a desire to know the truth of the "WORD OF GOD." They have been taught for centuries now, to ignore the written bible and never to listen to teachings of "GOD" in the bible. Many diverse societies have been established on the teachings which exclude the deity of "GOD THE FATHER; GOD THE SON; AND OF GOD THE HOLY GHOST."

In many of my writings, references have been made mentioning this behavior of people all over the world, of which is very crucial to the cause that so many souls have been lost and are bound for eternal destruction.

So I won't deeply submerse my dialogue into this issue of discussion, as I have already previously done so in other books.

In the historical enlightenment of the existence of "GOD," the one thing that we have learned and have come to understand, is that not only have "GOD" spoken to humanity before; but even more-so through the things which do appear in our present circumstances and situations and happenstances. Many, if not most of these things, "GOD" presently uses them to speak to humanity.

While so many religious organizations and denominational affiliations argue consistently as to whether "GOD" yet speaks audibly to mankind any more, many of the leadership heads have gone to great lengths to scientifically prove that it is no longer possible for "GOD'S" voice to be heard in these latter times of our human existence?

I must admit that I am rather amused, and even some-

Introduction

times amazed, when those who are determined to prove that *"God"* doesn't speak, when they desperately attempt to demand that *"God"* speak to them! They want immediate answers to questions, and solutions to problems. They want to know why their plans in the earth have failed so drastically.

To watch news media, and Internet media platforms, seeing these like people give unprecedented reasoning for which they have determined that *"God"* never spoke up for, or to them, is hysterical at best! Thinking themselves wise, they have become quite foolish. The "Sovereignty of God" places Him far above being accountable to mere men and women of the earth.

As it is, most people only desire to hear the *"voice of God"* speaking to comfort them, only after they had made the most embarrassing painfully disgusting mess of their lives! On their own selfish desires to do things their own way!

Throughout all of the historical reign of mankind in the earth, we have seen the distressing despair of man painfully struggling to understand the abstract *"silence of God"* in the midst of their own more aggravating circumstances.

People are led to believed by way of erroneous teachings in the churches and many media ministries, that we have been given the ability to instruct *"God"* in how to care for us, and to act on our behalf. Most are studiers and researchers of the *"speaking authority of Jesus Christ"* as He walked the earth, and of the *"spoken word of God"* throughout all of the recorded history of the bible.

This book my friend, is designated to encourage any reader to take more of an exhaustive, deeper expansive look into the realistic *"Silence of God!"* Which has been the experience for many, if not for most of us all. So many of us all have had the occasions in our lives to wonder, or even to ask the question; *"God where are you?"*

XIII

The Sovereignty of God's Silence

To understand the message of *"His silence."* To discern the meaning in the timing in the *"silence of God,"* whenever He appear to not speak in your life. *"Where is God?"* Why did *"God"* allow this to happen to me? Why is *"God"* letting the people of this world get away with sinning against the *"word of God,"* written in the bible? Doesn't *"God"* see child abuse, rape, same-sex marriages, and all of the talk against the churches?

These are only a few of the reasons given for me to write this book on the "Silence of God" for us, who walk this walk of faith, truth and of trust in the *"Lord."* My friend, even *"Jesus Christ"* asked the question on the cross; "My God, Why Have You Forsaken Me?" Even in the life of *"God's"* dear son, in the most important time of His sacrifice on the cross, *"God"* silenced Himself.

The "Silence of God" is as powerful and equally Anointed, as it is in these times of which we are made aware that it is truly "God" for truth, speaking to us and moving in our midst. Only the truth is that most people who should be listening while He is speaking to us, they have turned a deaf ear to *"the voice and to the messages of God."* They choose to only listen for *the voice or to the word of* "God" whenever they are in trouble.

Those who have been shameless as it relates to publicly speaking as the *"spirit of the Lord"* gives them the utterance, have silenced their mouths from speaking and have quenched *"the spirit of the Lord"* in the midst of unbelieving people of the world. Even though they are at the gathering of the churches!

Many who have received the awesome infilling of Holy Ghost(spirit) with the gift of speaking in tongues, have been influenced to question whether or not it is *"God"* speaking in and through them.

It has been stated by many, that those of us who speak in

Introduction

tongues in the services of the churches, claiming that it is "God" indeed speaking through us, that we are an annoyance to the flow of the services. I have also been made aware that it is likewise unreasonably annoying to those who desire to hear "God" speaking through us, whenever we are silent in the churches! They have not come into the services to come before "God" to hear silence. Yea, the plot thickens! The very people that often say nothing for the "Lord," are desiring to hear something from the "Lord!"

Many of the leaders in the churches who demand silence from the people in the pews, have not as of yet themselves learned to be silent! It is of no consequence to attend service only to sit underneath a teacher or a minister of the "gospel of God," who have proven to have nothing at all to say to the people in the audience to build their knowledge of faith, and of trust to live for the "Lord."

There is a time for silence! Even to those of us that have truly been called of "God," to speak truth to this dying world. I believe that if we indeed want "*the people of God*" to do according to what we teach them to do, then we as the leaders ought to be actual living examples of what we are teaching, so that they can see clearly what it is that we are asking of them!

Well, it is often quite easily assessed as to the reasons that we as people ought to indeed be quiet, silent, soundless, or speechless if you would prefer. It has often been the case that people are talking when they indeed ought to be listening. We can't all talk at the same time and learn things as we ought to be learning. Silence most definitely has it's place among us!

Many who may feel indeed that they have become more knowledgeable about praying to "God," have also led themselves to believe that "God" is now forced to respond to their prayers.

The Sovereignty of God's Silence

It has been bewildering, mind boggling, inexplicable and devoid of reasonable understanding that *"GOD"* would be silent in the midst of what is thought to be the faithful sentimental cries, in the midst of our human disparages.

For Him not to talk to us, or for Him not to make a move that would change the scope of things in our discombobulated realities, is spiritually assassinating for many. Many who never exercised faith in *"GOD,"* will almost never for certain adhere to *"FAITH IN GOD!"* Citing the misguided reasoning for which *"GOD"* was indeed silent when they came to the conclusion that they needed Him.

A most realistic truth is that *"GOD"* is very often silent when we ourselves are hard pressed in reaching out to Him in prayer. In truth, people would not be asking the questions of *"GOD's"* silence, were it not the truth! He had indeed held His peace while we His people demanded that He would be pleased to move for us!

"GOD" silenced Himself, while the children of Israel were in bondage to the Egyptian rule, 400 years, before *"GOD"* chose to answer their cries to be freed from their bondage. Throughout the Old Testament, on many occasions, *"GOD"* was silent while the people were threatened with exile, bondage, wars, and of the famines in the land.

We have been made aware that between the Old Testament and the writing of the New Testament, there were 400 years of silence! While we bask in the awesome manifestation of the plan of *"GOD"* for all mankind in the earth, we often overlook the fact that mankind almost convinced themselves, that *"GOD"* had left us all alone here in the earth.

"GOD" wasn't gone and neither had He lost an ability to speak to us in the earth. *"GOD"* clearly had a plan for man far beyond human comprehensive reasoning. Wonder? Just how many sermons have you heard about the years of silence?

Many messages are gleaned from the books of MALA-

Introduction

chi, and then of course from Matthew. But, what could the messengers of the "gospel of God" say to you when in fact there is nothing written for them to say, speaking about the suggested absence and of the "Silence of God," for 400 years.

Although "God" did indeed speak again to mankind, He has often since sprinkled humanity with the enigma of His silence! Many people have gone over the edges of life and of living, citing hopelessness and despair, believing that there is no way that they can make it without the "Lord." They think as a result, that they know that He is not going to help them, simply because He's been too silent, concerning their need.

What a blessing it is to be able to have this discussion on "The "Sovereignty of God's Silence." I have been trusted to challenge the mentalities of the people in the churches and the communities, to cause them to think more soberly and to be faithfully adherent trusting in the "Lord," even though at times He can't be traced!

Come now and let us reason together, we will rationally approach the truthfulness of "God's" silence. Yes, you do want to know why "God" has been silent whenever it was discovered that He indeed had held back from speaking to you, and or for even moving on your behalf.

Perhaps you've been seeking answers, and or in need of certain solutions, be advised that it is way too soon to give up on "God!" Don't throw in the towel, and don't get up off of your knees praying!

"God" knows what He's doing, and He knows what He's doing with you and me. Tune in to Him and listen more clearly for His un-mistaken voice. The power of "God's" silence can actually blow you away! Were it not for the grace and the mercy of God, His silence would burst our eardrums.

Note: Just because you have not heard Him, doesn't nec-

The Sovereignty of God's Silence

essarily mean that He is not speaking, nor that He has not spoken already! Let's see...

Chapter 1

Generation of Too Much Noise

And they heard the voice of the Lord God walking in the garden in the cool of the day: and Adam and his wife hid themselves from the presence of the Lord God among the trees of the garden.   Genesis 3:8; Make a joyful noise unto the Lord.   Psalms 100:1

NOISY DISTRACTIONS FROM THE SANCTUARY

If, when we being spiritually attuned to the frequency of God's spirit, and sensitive to the power of the word of God; we live to know the distinction of the sound of God's voice. The very voice of God flows through the sovereign spirit of God. His presence, brings about the certainty of His unmistakable sound throughout all of the realm of the earth.

As we allow ourselves to listen closely to the specific sounds and raised volumes of noises among the crowds of people at any gathering, the spontaneous conclusion within the faculties of our reasoning, is that these noises all bear specific meanings and intended purposes. Every other sound outside of the voice of God, has but only the ability to speak of it's allowed existence, to reveal its true identity.

We are made aware of many diverse things, knowing to call them by their names. As the result of the sounds that they make among our living atmospheres, they identify themselves. At other times the sounds leave us wondering to define the distinction of the origin, to determine the actuality of it.

We hear so much noise in the sanctuaries now, only be-

The Sovereignty of God's Silence

cause many of the people nowadays have chosen to create noisier atmospheres in the sanctuary of the churches. Excitement of noise have been mistaken to represent that the presence of the Lord has filled the sanctuary.

However, to the spiritually aware, word literate people in the churches, who are indeed spirit filled, it is become only an atmosphere filled with noise! Noise, in and of itself, around the churches, have been made to be indistinguishable! Preferred noise does not at all bespeak of the desire for the people to be in the presence of the Lord!

It is of grave necessity that every individual come to know and to distinguish the presence of the Lord, clearly, to hear His voice! We always need to know what is the spirit, and the difference in what indeed is not the spirit of the Lord!

Carnal minded, common, worldly thinking people associated to the commonwealth of the churches, are more easily intrigued to accept excitement and emotional expressions of noise making in the sanctuary, as being pleasing to the Lord.

So many people appear to be paralyzed and put on mute, in the true actual presence of the Lord. As we of the churches begin to praise and to worship God in the spirit and in truth, there is a vast number among the gathering of the people in the churches who are sort of left behind! They are left out of the spiritual dialogue with God!

They become spectators and visitors viewing the services, rather than being active participators in worship. I know that it is easier to get involved and to make noise with the crowd of unsure religious church goers, who have no relationship with the Lord!

We have got to know when and of what to respond to in the churches. It could be a spiritual death sentence to miss out on responding to the spirit of the Lord! It is also not good to just allow all types of noise to take place during the services of the churches.

Generation of Too Much Noise

While simultaneously ignoring the significance of certain noises until they are threating the safety and the welfare of our space of existence, we just may live to regret the day and the times that we did not respond to the sound of the noises being made around us?

Truth is, there is way too much noise pollution around us everyday! There is noise that we absolutely need, and then there is noise that we could definitely do without.

We all are commonly endowed with the sharpened resolution of our minds, to accurately pinpoint many factors of noise in our atmospheric surroundings. Subsequently, we expect some sort of noise wherever we go, and we often prefer noisier surroundings. Rather than the stilled silence of quietness, as result of the emptiness in the present atmosphere, absent of noise making people. "(*As in a Cemetery*)"

I could go on for a number of years naming the different noises, and I would still not be able to name them all! Noises are too vast, multifaceted and very necessary to us, as we actually develop our human existence on the earth.

As we learn to hear and to distinguish the noises that we have heard in our hearing, we scrutinize the sounds to capture a memorable distinction to mark a dependable recognition of all sounds made. The noise of specific sounds aid us in the development of skills and certain abilities.

To be clueless and unaware of the noises, will not aid us in making a decision, and will often leave us defenseless as pertaining to our actions or reactions in direct response to the messages that are being delivered to us, by the noise.

Noise is often used to drown out any messages of speech that people are not willing to hear. Sinful people are not willing to hear the messages in the word of God, when the truth is spoken. They often flee the presence of God, to noisier ungodly atmospheres that will drown out the message and silence the power of the truth to command a change in

The Sovereignty of God's Silence

one's life.

Of these latter generations, many people prefer the noise of political rallies, up-rises against the police, and for all types of racial divides. Of course we are aware that the preference for the noise of the partier have not been silenced. Any factor of noise that doesn't worship God in spirit and in truth, is preferred.

ON THE PARTIER SIDE

This present generation of people have outright preferred the degrading lyrics and the redundant rhythmic noise of the DJ over the microphone, over and against the spoken word of God, preached or prophetically uttered in the church, likewise also spoken over the microphone.

They want noisy atmospheres equivalent to that of nightclubs and parties that allows for them to shake and to twist their behinds.

People want excitement and entertainment, having cited the church and holy living as boring and dull. People pay to be a part of the noise going on at the clubs. It seems to me that most of the leaders of the churches across the board are in agreement with the people. All they want is for the people to pay to make some noise, though devoid of the joy of the Lord!

Pentecostal based churches and many of the Baptist churches, as well as Non-Denominational congregations have always been of the noisier crowds to gather in the churches for worship services. They all seemed to embrace *PSALMS 100:1; "Make a joyful noise unto the Lord."*

They made a joyful noise to the Lord as they danced in the spirit. They danced a victorious dance, to songs of victory. They were witnesses to the spirit of the Lord manifesting in the services, where they also witnessed deliverance, and miraculous healing!

They experienced demons being cast out of demon pos-

Generation of Too Much Noise

sessed people. Specially, they were endowed with the anointing to discern the noise of the spirit of the Lord, in contrast to the noise of any satanic infiltration from the outside influences against the assembly of the services.

Iniquity and selfishness has increased to an outpouring rage against the move of God, right in the aisles of the churches! Most people, being disconnected to the spirit of God, have thrown in the towel on walking by faith in God, and have given up on pleasing the Lord.

Too often the noise being made in the churches have no benefit to the people in attendance. They think that just because they showed up for the service, it ought to be enough to satisfy God. After all they did get involved in making the noise of the service, they just might be led to believe?

Just back a few decades ago, whenever the church atmosphere became noisy, as the people opened their mouths to worship and to praise God, something mighty would happen in the spirits of the people, that would cause their lives to never be the same.

Now the churches make their own specified noises expecting for God to show up and join in the party, if He would prefer to do so? It is obvious that the people of the churches have determined in their own minds that if God doesn't like the party atmosphere and the noise that is being made, He can just stay away.

They have convinced themselves that they can take it from here. They make lots of unfounded noise, singing songs that don't even reverence the glory and the presence of God. Yet, whenever the need truly arises for the presence of God, whereas a word is needed from the Lord, they expect for God to just jump in from wherever He might be, to join in as if to be excited about an opportunity to be on the program!

Although the churches, many of them anyway, never really hunger for the absolute truth to be spoken from the word

The Sovereignty of God's Silence

of God. They want some sort of a word spoken that they can apply God's name to it? Seems like they make noise to see if they can be heard outside of the windows of heaven? Perhaps they expect for God to look out of the windows of heaven, and recognize their noisy efforts? *Genesis 11:5-6;*

The noise of the services of today are purported to be for the sake of reaching the younger generation of people, for the Lord. However, the same younger generations are coming to the churches while yet attending the nightclubs and the parties, just as they were doing before coming to the church.

This generation's element of noise in the churches, draws people to the churches, but it fails to bring them into desiring "Christ Jesus" to be their "(Lord and Savior!)"

The adapted noise of this age suggest to the people that they can have this life of salvation in "Christ Jesus", and that same life of sin and of shame of living in the world. While the word of God clearly commands that we leave the world of sin, to come into the life of "Christ", through faith.

Today's noise is both confusing and deceptive. It sounds like the people of the churches are having an experience in the presence of God. Only you will often find that there is no moving of the spirit of the Lord in the services. There is just a lot of flesh on parade, as the true motive is to be seen of men; but, never mind God!

In God, it is not even possible to be depraved of having the good time in the Lord, which has been previously ordained for us! Being saved and delivered is of the greatest experience that everyone of us could ever have while living on the earth. It was never intended for us, just to have a good sociable time, dancing and partying at the church!

What many people had never considered, was that, we made a joyful noise while at the churches, because of the wonderful presence of the Almighty God! Which can never be compared to any other idea of a religious deity. No oth-

Generation of Too Much Noise

er expression of entertainment or religion, could even come close to the awesomeness of God's glorious presence!

The people of the world, living in their sin and shame, used to keep their desired expression of noise away from the sanctuary of the churches. They, even in their sin, had a since of respect for the power of the presence of God. I loved the fact that the people of the world, knew the difference.

They were made aware of the differences in the people of God through their demeanor and their lifestyles, after they had left he fellowship of the church. Many of the people of God, were living the life of truth and righteousness. They were not at all trying to mix with the world, as they intended to please the Lord with their lives!

TALKING NOISE

So many people from the leadership to the laymen, from the pulpit to the pews, they talk way too much, both in the churches and in their personal lives. They are always bragging about everything that they have acquired, their jobs, their accomplishments, and even about their churches.

You would not even be led to believe that God had any responsibility with their lives. Right over the public address system, they are heard speaking as if they are talking to a group of investors at a country club, at a comedy club, or in a financial group seminar.

You may ask;"WELL WHAT'S WRONG WITH THAT?" I ask you; "WHAT'S RIGHT WITH THAT?"

These types of messages are taking place right in the sanctuary where people should be being taught the word of God. That particular resource of information has a designated time and place for the benefit of entertainment, and enhancements of the people, for advancements. But, that's at best, making nothing but noise in the churches!

Messages that center on stuff and the acquisition of things and political agendas, are immaterial to the actual plan of

The Sovereignty of God's Silence

salvation and to the purpose of living holy in our daily lives. Whenever we drive down a street or even if we are riding the bus, we clearly see where to acquire things and lots of stuff as we pass so many stores and businesses.

You will also see lots of advertisements, suggesting who to vote for, and of where to go and to cast your vote. The reason the world have slipped into such greater disparage, is simply because the people have placed their trust in Politicians. "*Ain't nobody God; But God!*"

The preachers have found it more befitting to preach about every other topic of discussion in the pulpits, everything else other than the message of "The Kingdom of God in Christ Jesus." The noise is all about money and sowing financial seeds. But, they don't want you to drop any noisy money in the offering pan. They want some quiet money!(Dollar Bills)

If it's not one thing, it's another. There have been a changing of the guard, whereas the former pastors and the Bishops are passed on to their graves. The younger generations pastors and the newly appointed Bishops, simply refused to gracefully be the successors of the past leaders, they have come in as "*hostile takeovers!*"

They are not at all so careful as to watch for the keeping of the landmark boundaries which had been established for the churches in the word of God. The noise of their messages is that the old way was too strict for the people of the churches. They are rather forward in telling the people of the churches now that God don't want them to live dull boring lives.

They say to the people, not to listen to ministers who preach strict messages, and the people are further admonished not to give financial support to those types of ministries. They are preaching from cartoons and from animated movie themes, such as; "The Lion King" and others.

They intend to lighten things up while they liven things

Generation of Too Much Noise

up during worship, so called, by raising the noise volumes. I agree that there is nothing worse than a dead church service where the presence of God is not there. However, raising the noise levels of the service alone, simply is never going to be the answer! Allow God into the services.

Not knowing or even understanding the metaphorical messages of the themes that these screen films are depicting, they are spewing the devils venom all over the sanctuary. Such noises from the pulpits aid the devil's agenda to hinder the seriousness of the spiritual growth and consistency of the people in the churches.

I hardly ever even allow myself to sleep in church, knowing that I am going to miss something for my soul. However many messages that I have sat under as of late, have sent me straight to the sleep zone. Many in the pulpits are talking loud, but they are actually really saying nothing to the souls of the people from the word of God.

Many people will say to you about certain preachers; "Oh They Can Bring The Mail." As my wife and I go out to the mailbox to get the mail delivered, we are often disappointed with all of the junk mail. Department stores or businesses are saying something in their mail delivery ads, but that mail is never saying anything directly to us about our livelihood. The advertisement is to anyone who retrieves it from the mailbox.

One of the greater dangers around the churches has been that everyone now has got something to say that usually appeases their own feelings and emotional desires! They don't like it God's way, according to the written word of God. Called or not, they want their voices heard. They are talking from places of positions to which they are never going to be of any true benefit to the body of Christ.

Many sermons are centered around an individual's family, hardly leaving any space to even mention the name of "Jesus

Christ." Leaders are preferring to have their family members in charge of things at the church, disregarding the members of the church who support the ministry, and are qualified to handle several offices of the ministry.

Cataclysmic clashes, unnecessarily as result of so much noise in the churches, is happening. Here it is! Many who clearly have never surrendered their lives to Christ, are in the pulpits leading as the pastors. They are pushing every agenda against the written word of God.

Their favorite messages are that, "Ain't Nobody Better Than Anybody Else." The truth is that God never calls for anybody to be better than they themselves are required to be through the written word of God. You ought to desire to be better than you were whenever you came into the Lord to be saved and set free from the life of sin.

To focus yourself on your own life in Christ, will cancel the need for you to make noise in comparison of yourself to everyone else, to anyone that will listen. The pride of noise is what displeases the Lord! Remember that God delights in a joyful noise! While God hates pride!

Whether you like it or not, God is a jealous God; He will have no other gods before Him. With all of that noise and bragging, you make yourselves a god. You want everyone else to look at you, while God wants all of us to look at His word, and to look to Him for all that we will ever need!

Quiet The Noise

It's way past the time to take control of the noise and of the noise makers. I have been in small churches that looked like to be about 20 x 20 ft in diameter, or smaller. They had a full band and an expensive PA system, and several microphones. Everything was blasting at full volume. No one payed attention to the scour on the faces of the people in the audience.

For some reason or another, the person on the micro-

Generation of Too Much Noise

phone seemed to have believed that the louder their voices were amplified, that it meant that they were truly projected as being anointed. Of course, I could have told them that they were truly annoying! They would be much better received if they would simply turn the volume of the microphone system down!

The guitarist played so loud, it was if he had forgotten that he was in fact in the church, instead of an open park, several miles broad and deep. His distorted guitar sounded as though it had fallen into the deep end of the ocean, but continued to play anyway.

The drummer played and banged so hard on the drums as if he were mad at the world, so he decided to take his anger out on the drums, right in the middle of the service. He were beating the drums as if there was no one else there besides himself!

The very sound of his lack of drumming skills turned into the desperate sounds of noise of an abusive event, just as if we were all right in the middle of the situation taking place.  These musicians seemed to have no respect for the use of volume pedals, neither of temperance of any sort. We were unable to appreciate the service for the unskillful performance of these musicians disturbing volumes.

As the person on the microphone would say; "Everybody Make Some Noise", just as though it was if they were shock with an electric chord or as if a grenade had been thrown in the mist of them, they responded in obedience to making noise as commanded! They all blew up!

That small church being packed to capacity, most everyone simultaneously began to raise their voices with the volumes of the musicians. The noise rattled the walls and deeply vibrated the bodies of the people in attendance. They thought it was the spirit of the Lord moving in the atmosphere, but it was definitely the vibration of the noise, shaking things up.

The Sovereignty of God's Silence

I am concerned that perhaps the leadership and the musician staff alike, had never been trained to control the volume levels in the sanctuary. If God was indeed speaking, not many would be able to clearly focus on Him for the sake of all of the noise. It's no wonder that in many of the churches, it is felt and mistakenly believed, that God has gone silent!

Get over yourselves! Church worship is never meant to be a race related experience! As God; is the God of every people across the universal globe, so also is the church intended to be for all people.

Tailor made to fit the particular community of people, to which the church has been planted, many people are deceived and led to believe that God is the God of their race of people, only.

It is intended that the people who come out to worship in the services at the church, that they are to have a true God experience in "Christ Jesus", through the power of the "Holy Ghost", every time!

If the people don't come to see you being used of God, they certainly should never need to come to the church just to see you perform and to keep making noise!

Calm yourselves, and let the people see the Lord at work in your church and in your life. Thank You!

Chapter 2

What Silences Him

He was oppressed, and He was afflicted, yet He opened not His mouth: He is brought as a lamb to the slaughter, and as a sheep before her shearers is dumb, so He openeth not His mouth. ISAIAH 53:7

STILL DON'T HAVE A CLUE

It intrigues me desperately, to challenge the unreasonable conclusions of your minds, suggesting that "God" is silent. Since before the beginning of time, of which we have been made aware through the aid of the scriptures, we have never found and we will never find that God has ever suffered any deficiency of speaking. Be advised that God does not have any fear or apprehension of speaking to man today!

God, in His deity, being so powerfully and creatively spoken authority, called everything known to mankind into existence. The eternal essence in the nature of "God" can never allow that anything spoken by "God" to be as if He were ever quiet! The eternal reign of "God's" word, will never fail throughout the entire existence of the earth and time!

Although created man has felt through the years, that they have made changes to void Whatever "God" said, things have happened and they will continue to happen just as He said that it would. "God's"; words are infallible, and His commands and promises are immutable!

Nothing and no one have the power to reverse, to invert or to ever nullify anything that "God" has ever spoken! I have come into contact with many people who were praying, trying to convince "God" to change His spoken word concerning them. I have heard many deliver sermons over the pulpits, who were attempting to dissuade the accepted validation of the truth revealed, written in the scriptures.

They were seeking to shift the exact meaning previously received and understood in the hearts and the minds of the people, from the teachings of the accounts witnessed in the scriptures.

Some have set under the instruction and the teaching of many confident, spirit filled teachers of the bible for years. Some had even gone as far as to study the scriptures for themselves, seeking to get a permanent grasp on the intended meaning of the messages of the bible. There is no possible way to prevent "God" from speaking, when people are determined to hear from Him, or not!

Too many people seem to forget just who it is that they are talking about whenever they speak in reference to "God." We need never to forget that "God" is not a man! His ways are not our ways! "God", is forever unmovable! It is totally impossible to eradicate the word of His mouth!

In the book of *"Genesis"*, "God" spoke and things as we know of them even to this very day, came into permanent existence. "God" spoke and the elements of the world fell into place, obeying the command of "God's" voice. For example: "God" is not still speaking to the moon, the stars and to the sun. He spoke and they have obeyed His command ever since.

Rain, sleet and snow, still fall from the clouds up in the sky. The storm clouds still rise, while the wind blows to deliver the great drops of rain all over the earth and the sea. Everything on the earth sways and moves in recognition and in respect to the powerful winds that blow.

Eagles and all sorts of fowl, fly through the air of the sky, flapping their powerful wings. Since from the beginning of

What Silences Him

creation, all on the created command of "God's" spoken word. They don't ask "God" each time that they take to the sky, if it would be okay for them to fly? "God" had already said what their wings were supposed to do. They obey His command!

The scripture informs us that when He spoke, it sounded like thunder, or the sound of many trumpets! His voice has been reported to have the sound of rushing mighty waters and of the power of great rushing mighty winds! Although He is likewise also accounted as to have spoken with a still small voice. Yet His voice was distinct and unmistakable, never to be confused with the sound of any other voice in existence.

Even when "God" speaks to us just above a whisper in our hearing, it is as powerful as a nuclear explosion moving things out of the way. Whenever He answers our prayers, the things that were standing in our way, causing all sorts of problems for us, are moved immediately! Locked doors and closed realities are opened unto us as result of His spoken answer to our faithful prayers.

DEAD AND NEITHER DEATH, SILENCES GOD

The voice of "God" is so powerful, that even the dead can hear Him speaking. According to the 37th chapter of *EZEKIEL;* an exceeding great army responded to the command of the prophet, after "God" had commanded him to prophesy to dead bones. The dead and dried out army stood upon their feet and lived, again the second time.

Ask those who are determined that "God" is now silent, to explain how it is that dead Lazarus, in the 11th chapter of *JOHN;* heard the voice of God calling him from the grave, and from death, after being dead four days already? Perhaps many people are too quick to discount "God's" ability to speak to us like the account of the scriptures report!

As we all know of death, the dead don't hear and neither are they privileged to know or to respond to anything, unless

The Sovereignty of God's Silence

God says so! I will give two examples of people that I knew of personally right here in Fort Worth, Texas. Although I had been made aware of several other accounts, that were called back from the dead.

FIRSTLY; ~ My biological father the Late William Thompson Sr. suffered an acute Asthma attack back in the summer of 1987. After being rushed to arrive in the hospital emergency! Laying there on the operating table in the emergency room, he coded 2 or 3 times and was placed on life support.

He would lay there unconscious for several days, of which after reviving, he confessed to having been brought before the presence of "God." He was dead as far as he knew of and confessed! After being spoken to by the *"SPIRIT OF GOD,"* he was commanded to go back and to continue living because it wasn't his appointed time to die yet. That once dead man lived again until April 6, 2000.

SECONDLY; ~ My late brother-in-law, Willie Dennis Barrette Jr; developed pneumonia and had to be hospitalized as result. He fell into a coma and would lay there basically clinically dead for 21 days. My wife and I went to the hospital to pray, I layed hands on him and anointed him with oil, in the name of *"JESUS CHRIST"!* He revived instantaneously, after a few days he reported to us that he had been before the presence of God, where he had seen many wonderful things to come.

There are so many other situations that I know of that happened like so. Whereas, the people reported to have been dead and in the presence of "God." Even the dead as we know of them, that had passed away from our world of living, according to documented reports, they have also confessed that they heard the voice of "God" speaking to them, and they lived again, as a result.

While so many people ascribe to the reversal of what is referred to as near death experiences, they give the power to that of medicine and to the medical professionals. So many people are not willing to ever believe that people have heard the voice of "God" speaking to them as they lay there in the very images of death, in the hospital under intensive care of medical professionals.

They'd rather believe that it couldn't have been possible that they were dead, because the machines and the medical attention kept them alive and breathing all of the time. Science determines to debunk the idea of there being another reality after the body has expired in death.

They say that nerves and the brain having final involuntary experiences? Even though an individual had never been a confessing believer in Jesus Christ. They were not even saved! That being the only explanation for what might have been seen and experienced, after a death had occurred.

As a teenager in the church one Sunday morning in the latter part of 1970's, I witnessed one of the elderly mothers of the church, expire right in the middle of the service! Others seated around her notice that she had collapsed and was unresponsive.

The people became rather emotionally shaken and they began to alert the leadership of the church. There were registered nurses who were members of the church, who were also in attendance during the service. The pastor order them to examine the elderly woman to see what was going on.

As they closely examined her, it was indeed reported that she had passed, as there were no vitals signs of life. The pastor commanded the church to be silent and went over to her and layed hands on the woman's forehead and began to command her to revive and to live in the name of *"JESUS CHRIST!"*

By the leading of the spirit, the late Supt. LC Castleberry called her back from the dead! Immediately, she began to raise her hands to the Lord to give Him praise. The mother woke up and began again to live right in the presence of all of the people there who witnessed it all take place!

It seemed to me, as if the entire church lifted up extreme radical praise to God, even as I had never seen them do before. All because that dead woman heard the voice of "God" commanding her to live again, and she did indeed live again! Not even death can silence the voice of "God." If you're spiritually dead, try listening for the voice of "God!" You will be made alive to live in *"Christ Jesus"*; forever more!

All people, every man, woman, boy, and girl; will hear and respond to the voice of "God" calling them from their graves. Don't worry, you won't need to worry about being able to explain hearing His voice, other than the fact that "God" has already spoken it in the written word of "God." Although you have accused "God" of being silent, You will hear Him speak on that great day. You Better Be Ready!

Why You Might Have Silenced Him

Many that accuse "God" of being silent, according to their own despairetive accounts, they have often done so for either 1 or 2 reasons? Firstly; they have not believed in *"Christ Jesus"* as being *"The only Begotten Son of God!"* Many are taught in other religious organizations to disregard and never to believe the story of *"Christ Jesus."* They simply don't even like to hear His name!

Even many who have personal accounts of what He has done for them, they still don't want to believe Him, for who He is! They confess that they don't even believe in "God." They say that "God;" somewhere up in the sky, somewhere out of this world, is only a myth.

They say that it can't be real! Get out of here with that! Yet when needed, they still can't seem to realize why they can't hear Him speak to them, although they have never changed their confessions, rejecting *"Christ Jesus."*

Secondly; those who purport now to having been saved and washed in the precious, shed blood, of Christ Jesus!

Who died on the cross at Calvary, out on Golgotha's hill! They have as of yet to totally develop and mature, since the time that they at first believed and confessed *"Christ Jesus"* with their own mouths.

It is necessary for people to grow in "Christ", to the point and fact of coming into the knowledge of who "God" is! According to the word and of the fullness of the *"Spirit of God."* People need desperately to be filled with the *"Holy Ghost!"* Until you have been filled with the spirit of the "Lord", through the indwelling presence of the "Holy Ghost", you will remain joyless.

Joylessness, is to the likes of being in a dead dank dry and cold grave. The messages of being saved alone, just as you are, without being filled with "Holy Ghost", is just an excuse and an house for allowing joylessness a place to live in your own soul. *"The joy of the Lord is your strength." Nehemiah 8:10;* Joy, is the strength you need in order to believe and to know that "God" speaks and that He is not at all silent! Or is He?

So many people have not yet, successfully adhered without any doubt, to true faith in "God"; as of the faith that pleases "God!" They have ideas of faith, that don't constitute connecting to "God", that will actually please the "Lord." *Hebrews 11:6;* People, rather, believe that they have that kind of faith which identifies with other people. Even if "God", doesn't approve or answer any prayer request for them.

They expect for "God" to just answer and or to speak to them anyway! Regardless of their lack of true faith. Because it is known that "God;" is all powerful and all knowing! People choose to feel that "God's" love is just too great for Him to disregard any of their needs or request. Many are determined to continue to do whatever they want to do, as it relates to sinning and living ungodly.

Remember, whenever "God" speaks, the wind and the sea

obey His voice. As *"Jesus Christ"* spoke to the wind and to the sea, commanding it to be seated and to be silent! He wasn't giving a new command to the wind and to the sea. He was simply reminding the wind and the sea for the sake of the disciples, of the created commands given from the beginning.

Faith, over their fear, would have allowed for the disciples to know of the originated position of command for the wind which was originally the air, and of the sea of which from the beginning was only the water.

The air became wind on the command of God's voice, whereas the air began to move about the earth's atmosphere, in every direction allowed by God. Air alone allows for the wings of eagles and of other birds to soar, and to sort of float across the sky effortless. However, the wind will require a more strenuous effort to navigate and to soar to desired elevations and destinations.

Water was indeed here in the beginning where it all began. The bible indicates to us that darkness was upon the face of the deep.(Water) In the beginning water had no obligations and neither did it have commission to sustain the aquatic life of fish and other marine life. Water in the earth, has been required for the refreshing of all the living creations upon the face of the earth, including for man.

"Christ Jesus" walked on the water, the same water that He is now speaking to, commanding it to calm, now as the sea. They were amazed and totally astonished, that *"Christ Jesus"* could and did speak to the sea. They marveled as the sea immediately responded as a well trained child will do when spoken to by a parent, or guardian. Hive voice is amazing.

"Christ Jesus" was walking on a journey with His disciples and He became hungry. He approached a fig tree in full bloom, full of leaves, but it bore absolutely no fruit. *"Jesus*

CHRIST"; being *Emanuel(God with us, in the flesh)* spoke to the deceptive tree and commanded that it would never bear fruit again.

He spoke to the now living tree in full bloom, just living and sashaying itself, as if it were ready to supply the fruit of it! But, the problem was that it was indeed blossomed out of season, as if being out of season never mattered to "God?" It had nothing but leaves, as it bore no fruit. It had nothing to offer to the *"LORD JESUS CHRIST"*, although it looked the part of being ready, indeed!

Within hours of returning from the journey, the tree had withered and dried up from the root, down in the ground, and was dead! In just less that 24 hours, on the spoken authoritative command of *"CHRIST JESUS."* The apostles of Christ were again astonished at the responsiveness to the spoken word of "CHRIST JESUS", to things in the earth's realm.

UNDERSTAND WHY HE'D BE SILENT

I know thy works, that thou art neither cold nor hot: I would thou wert cold or hot. So then because thou art lukewarm, and neither cold nor hot, I will spew thee out of my mouth. REVELATION 3:15-16;

"God" knows exactly who we all are and He's aware of the spiritual sate that we are in. Somehow we the people of the churches have been duped into believing that we have secret passage with "God" simply because we are members of the church.

Dangerously unaware of the things to come just ahead of us, we go on and on, as if to be living in the righteousness of "God", walking by faith. When in fact, many are often only members of the local churches. Often being people who never even follow or obey the teaching from the leadership in the church.

Many and most of the people who attend church have

never even learned the scriptures. They adamantly refuse to attend a prayer service, citing that they can pray at home, and of course they should indeed pray at home and everywhere else.

Church attendance is now received as nothing more than religious entertainment. Each week the people are prepared for the Sunday morning show at the church. Covid-19; did quite the job in exposing who the real people of the churches really are. Many who had fallen away and quit attending the services, have stopped any activity of things related to the church, all together.

I could go on and on about who is to blame for the people not being interested in the churches, as it relates to the parishioners and the pastors, but to no avail. Everyone wants to have someone else to blame for their short comings.

This strong word of admonishment written in the book of REVELATION, has been here all along. This is not new! However it has been greatly ignored and disregarded as a word of warning to the people of the churches worldwide.

"God" says; *that I would that you were either cold or hot!* Here's why! God speaks to the cold persons to get them ignited on fire, to change them! Acquainting them with the powerful presence and spirit of God! He's the answer whenever you do not know how to turn your lives over to Him.

When you are living in sin, fully and completely unaware of change in your life, sometimes not even knowing that you may need change, *"CHRIST JESUS"* is the answer! He's the only way to really ever change from the darkness to the light. Others who are willfully living in sin will give you a sinful pass to continue living in the ways that you are indeed living.

You are living in the cold winter of your life where nothing of any real true substance will grow. You may cheat and finagle your way in and through life, to have everything that your heart ever desire. However, the joy and the happiness

What Silences Him

which escapes you consistently, can only come to you as result of living in the Lord. *II Corinthians 5:17;*

"God" speaks to those who are indeed hot, because they are ignited of the *"Holy Ghost"*, already! The hot are those who have developed relationship with the "Lord" and in constant fellowship of the spirit, through the *"Holy Ghost."* Daily their determination is to be in prayerful dialogue with the *"Father in Heaven."*

The hot are determined to win the lost for *"Christ Jesus"*, even if they never attend the personal churches of their own choices. They care to increase the *"Kingdom Of God"*, bringing as many as possible into the fellowship of the spirit of the *"Living Lord."* They know that *"Christ Jesus"* is *"Lord"* and the *"Savior"* of the world! And they are never ashamed to let the world know.

The hot are seeking the *"Lord"* daily through the word of "God." They are consistently turning the pages of the bible seeking for the total clarity of the scriptures. They know the need of a clear and comprehensive understanding in the word of "God", for the sake of being able to rightfully divide the word. *II Timothy 2:15;*

The hot are not found spending the very best of their quality time recreating, and keeping up with the current events of the word. They trust "God" in everything concerning their lives here on the earth, until "God" says the time is up. The hot, have learned to wait on the *"Lord!"* Until He brings the things that we have desired to pass.

Another of the greater attributes of the hot, is that they are not living in fear! They set themselves to live by faith in "God," no matter what! We all know that things will happen in our lives, but it better serves us to be prepared by being prayed up. The hot have designated prayer times to come before the *"Lord"* to meet Him at the throne.

Them that are indeed hot in the *"Lord"*, know that there

is no better place to be informed and increased, than in the presence of the *"Lord."* They refuse to compromise their status in the *"Lord"* for the sake of things and stuff that will all pass away in the process of time. They have the good since of knowing that only what you do for *"Christ"* will last.

Getting to know of the greater things of "God" will only come as result of being ignited on fire for "God." Doesn't matter how far and or how deeply you may go in studies of the bible. Or even in a religious class to study the origin of "God." And of all the things that He has made on the face of the entire planet. You only get to know "God"; and of all of the things that He has for all of us, through being born again, in "God!"

Now the lukewarm are total left out! "God"; IS Word!

John 1:1-5; Everything that "God" has done, has been done by and through the word of His mouth. Lukewarm people, sadly, will miss the manifesting awesomeness of "God." God indeed is a spirit, and He speaks. But, the spirit of "God" commands the word, the word commands the spirit man on the inside of us. There is absolutely nothing that we can do in the *"Lord"* without the aid of the spirit.

Everything else that we do is done of our own spirit, will, and desire. So many people want to hold "God" responsible for the failure of the things that they have done of their own will! He had nothing at all to do with those things. Lukewarm people are often busy thinking that they are doing things for "God?" Recklessly, they convince themselves that they have the right to choose whatever it is that want to do for the "Lord." We could all choose if that were all it takes to do things for "God."

Lukewarm people are those who know that they ought to indeed be hot! They are aware of what "God" is requiring of those of us who confess the name of *"Christ."* They all have been taught, or at least they have heard that it has been said, that "God;" is calling whom He desires! He knows what He wants us all to do, individually.

Your ears can't hear "God" calling you. You have got to tune in through the *"Spirit of "God"* to hear Him. Only then will you indeed know whether or not He is silent!

Lukewarm people are they who purposefully tend to ignore the tug of the spirit. The know how to silence the voice of the spirit of the Lord calling them out of sin, and into the marvelous light. Just as the lukewarm people ignore the spirit of the Lord, the scripture also admonishes us that God will spew them out of His mouth.

God will ignore them also! No one can ever beat God at that game of ignoring the voice of the call!

Chapter 3

God's Word: Spoken and Written

And God Said; Genesis 1:
For ever, O Lord, thy word is settled in heaven.
PSALMS 119:89;
God, who at sundry times and in divers manners spake in times past unto the fathers by the prophets,
HEBREWS 1:1;
My little children, these things write I unto you, that ye sin not. And if any man sin, we have an advocate with the Father, Jesus Christ the righteous.
I JOHN 2:1;

GOD; SAID IT BEFORE HE DID IT

What is it that "God's" word declares as being ungodly? Are you a part of it? Do you act and behave in such the manner that causes you to be recognized as ungodly before the "Lord?" Have you even come to terms with accepting the truth about ungodliness and of all unrighteousness?

Do you even understand why it is that "God" is so displeased with ungodliness? Why should it even matter to "God" that people choose not to do things like the bible says for them to be done? Perhaps you say, what's the big deal, that people have chosen their own ways of doing things without "God's" influence?

On the one hand, many people are saying that "God's" ways are outdated, and old. On the other hand when people are asked to change their ways of doing things, they say that they have been dong things in this way for many years now. They go back for many generations of their family's historical records, citing that they had seen their great~great~grandparents, and on up to their own parents do things this way! Don't really see the need for any changes to be made.

Maybe you're one of the people who choose to believe that "God" is just the big bully in the sky? You're all swollen on the inside of yourselves, because of the death of your loved ones. "God" seems so unfair, that He would touch the lives of your family members? It doesn't really matter that He has also touched the lives of all of our family members at one time or another!

You're so angry and disappointed that you didn't get to marry the person or your choice. You never got the job that you wanted. You didn't get to attend college, so now you don't have a degree. You asked "God" a question and He did not even think enough of you to give you an answer; you say?

You think that you should have been chosen as the pastor of the church. You don't know why the people don't like you. You can't see the trees for looking at the forest. Yet, you can't see the whole picture for looking at the object in the picture. Somehow you seem to get swallowed up of the things of life which matters the least, while you totally miss the things which matters the very most!

All of these things are but deflections to the proper responses to the written word of "God." The heart of many people are turned away from "God" through His written word. Yet, there is still a since of expectation from God! Concerning the welfare of human existence in the earth. You expect the same "God" in whom you care the very least for, if not at all, to care the very most for you!

While people have hardened their hearts and have turned away their hearing from the mouth of "God," through His messengers, people are often heard asking, where is "God?" Why didn't "God?" How is "God" going to do it? Why did "God" let this happen to me? How could "God" allow people to treat me this way?

As adamant as you have been in suggesting that you didn't need "God," how is it that you now find it even possible to blame "God" for your life? The things that are happening to you, most of it, you have brought it upon your own selves! Now it's about time that somebody told you the truth about you!

It is no wonder that "God" would neither talk to you, answer the prayers that you pray, or even give instructions to you for guidance along your way through life. It is oxymoronicly unintelligent to expect for "God" to do anything for you, when you never even desire to hear anything that He has spoken already in the written word of "God."

Hearing the spoken word, according to what has indeed been written and penned to the pages of the holy bible, will reveal to you that "God" has already done what you have been asking for Him to do for you. Your obedient response to His spoken word is the only way that you are going to be able to receive and to be blessed to have *"The Lord's"* truest blessings in your life.

Maybe it's that you never minded hearing the things that you wanted to hear concerning your needs? You just never cared to read of the fact that "God" doesn't approve of your own ways of living and of doing things! "God's" way is the best way for humanity! His way is the only way for those of us who intend to live eternally with "God" in Heaven!

When we read the word of "God," we are soon informed of the fact that "God" spoke and He said, then He did what He said, that was previously spoken! "God" does not only have the last say so, but He has the first say so! "God's" say matters the most! Whatever "God" says is right, and He's right the first time! "God" has the only say that matters!

As people of the earth, most of us would prefer that "God" would do what ever we ask of Him, but never have a say on the matter. Only, many people fail to realize that "God" will not be pushed around and told what to do. He can never be told to do whatever we ask and sit down and to shut up! He cares way too much for that!

I may be different from a lot of other people, but anyone that I don't even want to talk to or to hear what they would have to say to me, I don't want them doing anything for me! Since I can't hear what they will have to say to me, I can't trust anything that might choose to do for me!

KNOWING THAT GOD KNOWS YOU

Communicable exchange is of the utmost importance when seeking assistance or the services of someone else. Lack of communication will often result in the loss of financial resources, and of course the wrong things may happen as result. I can never receive from you, that of which I have not even asked of you! You can't just do whatever you want to do for me, having never asked if I wanted you to do it for me. Expecting for me to be satisfied, simply because you did it!

The truth is that, "God" knows everything, but you have got to ask for whatever it is that you want from Him. "God" has to know that you have asked for Him to do things for you. Many people are walking around needing and wanting things from the "Lord," but they are also refusing to ask. Just imagine that! *MATTHEW 6:33;*

So many others are having conversations within themselves, determining that "God's" requirements are too much for them to surrender to. Many people are still convinced in their own minds that the bible is too strict for people to live by. They want "God" to relax a bit and just go ahead and do things for people.

Don't let the devil or anyone else convince you that "God" just be [*tripping*]. No my friends, "God" means whatever He says, and you had better know that His word is final! It will definitely bless you indeed, if you were to step aside from

God's Word: Spoken And Written

your own opinion of "God's" word, to accept the fact that "God" is not going to change His word for anyone.

As important as you might have convinced yourselves that you are, you would be blown away to realize that you are even more important and special to "God." More than anything that you could ever imagine! "God" sees us, and He is totally aware of our needs. Even though we may often fail to see Him, through the "EYES OF FAITH" in "God."

Faith, is not a suggestion, faith is a necessary requirement. It is only through faith that we are ever going to get "God" to satisfy the longings of our hearts. Faith, is "God's" system for connecting us to His ways of doing things for us here in the earth. You can find the methods and the reality of faith written in the word of "God."

Read the "WRITTEN WORD OF GOD" in the "HOLY BIBLE," there you will be made aware of where to find "God," whenever you need HIM. "God" has said it; concerning humanity in the earth, no matter what you may think! "God" is going to do it simply because He has said it!

There are some things that just might seem to be impossible for "God" to do for anyone. But, the bible declares, there is nothing too hard for "God" to do! "God" can, and "God" will do it just for you and for me. You must be sincere in your hearts towards "God." Don't just attempt to try and test "God" to see if He will do it just because you asked for Him to do it.

"God" is ever on high alert concerning "HIS CHILDREN." He knows when our cries are genuine, and when we are just determined to attract His attention, for no reason at all. We don't get the attention of "God" for the sake of impressing one another. No matter how bad you want others to know that you have "God" in your lives, making a fowl cry will not be the proper manner of showing forth the "PRESENCE OF GOD" in our lives.

"God" desires to be seen of others in your lives, but He wants you to trust Him to shine forth as you give Him the praise and the glory! Worship Him for who He is, and not for just whatever He has done in your life. Don't worship and praise "God" to impress Him to see what you can get from Him as a result. This is not at all meant to be a things motivated kind of relationship between us and "God." It is for us to have a Love motivated relationship with Him.

God Inspired Men To Write The Bible

So many of the questions concerning the writing of bible, in general, they are asinine. The questions are geared towards turning the hearts of people away from hearing the word, to rely on the written data. Many of those who reject the written word, don't have reasonable alternatives. They'd just rather that others didn't believe "God" or the "*WRITTEN BIBLE.*"

They have developed foolish ideologies for rejecting the "*WRITTEN WORD OF GOD,*" that often makes since only to themselves. I am rather amused whenever I hear the statement that men wrote the bible. You might even be led to think that according to these people's attitudes, man is the very worst of "God's" creation? Could that be your thinking?

They have been so deceived, as a precedence they have it to be known of all people that they do not trust in man; or other people! As if they would have been more trusting of the bible, had it been written by aliens, instead? Yet, these same people seem to find themselves in agreement to the agendas that are totally contrary to the written mandates of the scripture, established by other men.

When other men say that evil is actually good for humanity, they agree. They say that there is nothing more befitting for the aid of settling the nerves of man like a stiff drink. Most people adhere to that kind of thinking. Most people even agree that there is too much religion in the world, however they never seek to establish a right relationship with the

Lord.

These things and so much more, the people of the earth seem to agree with, but they don't agree with "God!" They are in total disagreement with the "WORD OF GOD." Somehow they have convinced themselves that the "WORD OF GOD" is so unnecessary for todays society.

Many people hate the sinful and the evil things that other people do! But, yet they still find it non-befitting for people to be told what to do, and how they ought to do those things. Clearly, the bible is our instruction manual for living here on the earth. Our now behavior, determines our future existence, after this life will have ended! Only, the bible can show us the way of salvation and life, to assure us of the future with "God" eternally.

I am of the opinion that "God" literally spoke the word into the spirit of the men who were ordained to write. "God" said it to them, and they began to write just as He spoke the word. I could really argue the point of not being able to know the heart of "God" without the aid of "God!" People overlook the "HEART OF GOD" concerning all mankind, while they spend time arguing the validity of the "WRITTEN WORD OF GOD."

Of all of the things written in the "WORD OF GOD," could you even imagine the things that "God" never even allowed to be written? Simple minded people think to themselves that they have seen and read of the totality of "God" within the 66 canonized books of the bible. There are things about "God" that could never be written! As the earth doesn't even have the language system of words to complete the description, or to explain His character.

GOD SHOWED THEM WHAT TO WRITE, OR NOT

You tell me; just which of you could ever successfully write about 'Heaven" giving an accurate description of the place, when you have never even been there? The Apostles; "PAUL",

AND "JOHN"(the Revelator); they both wrote about "Heaven." They reported to have been caught up there to be with "God" in the spirit realm. Though, yet living in their own human existence.

They both reported seeing things to wonderful for the human skill of transcribing any written accounts! They saw things that no human language could ever describe. They saw created beings that were not at all human. They heard conversations and languages that were never heard of spoken on the earth by any people.

They wrote of things to come in the future existence of all man kind, for which we are now warned of. Most people absolutely fear reading the book of Revelation. Perhaps they even feel that if they never read that particular book of the bible, that just maybe they can thwart the very plan of "God" for the future of humanity.

Those things written, will surely come to pass, with total accuracy to the written accounts of the writers. Everything that they were given to write for us, is not at all hypothetical or fictitious! The witnessed accounts are realistic and they are true. The hosts of "Heaven" worshiped and praised "God" in the beauty of "His Holiness" as never before witnessed in all of the realm of the earth.

However, they also wrote of the beauty and the splendor of *"HEAVEN"* itself. They wrote of the atmospheric worship and the total cooperative agreement among all of the host of "Heaven." Nothing in "Heaven" was out of order, neither out of place. All of the "hosts of Heaven" knew their places and did their part as they were created to do.

"John" saw the *"LAMB OF GOD"* as if it were slain. "John" said; *"I BEGAN TO WEEP!"* One of the angelic host of "Heaven" said to "John;" *"don't weep for the Lamb which was slain, has prevailed and have won the victory."* The lamb is alive and well for us all. As "John" had begun to write, he was instruct-

God's Word: Spoken And Written

ed not to write some of the things of which he had seen. You should listen and be informed of the fact that there are some things about "Heaven," and many things about "God," that we will never know until we are there present with "God!"

They were released back into the natural realm among the rest of humanity of the earth, in their own natural bodies. It's written in the scripture; so many are not aware because they have never read the biblical accounts of these two *"Apostles of Christ."*

No man on the face of the planet, would have the knowledgeable scope of reasoning to write spiritually infused words, that appear to leap right off of the pages as we read them, all by themselves without the aid of the *"Spirit of God."* Now from "Genesis," to the book of "Revelation;" we hear the "voice of God" telling mankind what to write of the many "mysteries of God."

The scriptures so wonderfully explains the mystical mysterious movement of "God" in the earth among mankind. The writers of the scripture recorded the witnessed accounts of the miraculous acts and the wonderful interventions of the spirit! What people had seen and had heard in amazement, right before their eyes, they would be made aware to always remember, that *"He Is God!"*

Don't Receive Him But Still Want him

After all of the rejection of the scripture that we are now witnessing among people, we still hear people complaining about the "silence of God!" Not understanding, that whatever "God" has already spoken is eternal, there is no need for Him to ever say again, what had already been said!

I urge all people to latch hold of the "written word of God" and lock it into their own hearts. We have to do just as "David" said and did in "Psalms" 119:11; He said; *"thy word have I hidden in my heart, that I might not sin against thee."*

"God" has awesomely provided for us to insure that we

never live a life displeasing to Him. We have all been taught that where there is a will, there is a way! I'm referring to a way that you and I are never going to be responsible for creating on our won. We are only required to walk in the way created for us. Stay in the way that's been affixed and established for us! "Proverbs" 14:12;

You will find that there in the way prepared for us, that is where "God" will most assuredly be heard speaking with us. You can't be out of the way with "God," and make living out of the way on a daily basis, expecting for "God" to be interested in hearing you speaking to Him! It is not intelligent at all to expect to hear "God" speaking to you, other than to warn you of the judgment to come as result of being out of the way with Him.

So you say that "God" has indeed been silent concerning you and your prayers to Him; what do you suppose that you could ever do about it? Can you force "God" to speak to you? Do you have the power to break the "silence of "God?" Can you even discern the "*voice of "God"* whenever He does begin to speak to you?

Do you know if He is going to speak in your ears, or to the spirit-man on the inside of you? Does He speak loudly, or will He be speaking softly?

According to the 14th chapter of "I Corinthians;" "God" would much rather that you and I speak mysteries to Him in the spirit. Perhaps He's been silent because you were supposed to have been talking to Him instead!

Chapter 4

Discerning God's Silence

But as it is written, Eye hath not seen, nor ear heard, neither hath it entered into the heart of man, the things which God hath prepared for them that love him. But God hath revealed them unto us by his Spirit: for the Spirit searcheth all things, yea, the deep things of God. For what man knoweth the things of a man, save the spirit of man which is in him? Even so the things of God knoweth no man, but the spirit of God. Now we have received, not the spirit of the world, but the spirit which is of God; that we might know the things that are freely given to us of God. Which things we also speak, not in the words which man's wisdom teacheth, but which the holy ghost teacheth; comparing spiritual with spiritual. But the natural man receiveth not the things of the spirit of God: for they are foolishness unto him; neither can he know them, because they are spiritually discerned.

I CORINTHIANS 2:9-14;

KNOWING WHAT DISCERNMENT IS

SPIRITUAL DISCERNMENT, ~ *"is the gifted ability of the spirit, which enables an individual to know what is either seen beyond what has been visualized; to clearly interpret what has been heard as result of a spoken word; and or even to decipher the true feelings of an emotion, a gesture or a touch."* APWTJ-2023

Discerning or discernment, must ever be recognized as an extraordinary attribute of the holy spirit. Discernment recognizes the spirit working in an individual or even the spirit of the person. Being gifted to discern will enable you to see beyond the mask, whenever those who are wearing masks, refuse to remove them. Discernment dives beneath the surface, all at the behest of the spirit of the Lord.

Discernment is more of an aggressive posture of spiritual authority, whereas those who possess the gifted ability might appear to be a bit zealous to look into the lives of others around them. It is an endowment that allows for one to see without any applied effort to look, or of a desire to know.

Those who are indeed filled with the "spirit of God," they ought to respect, as well as to appreciate, the openness of the "spirit of God." Which enables them to see beyond the natural realm, into the realm of the spirit. Discernment also establishes the ability to attune the frequency of an individual's hearing. Far beyond the stratus sphere, into an atmosphere where no natural ability of hearing can ever be operable.

The average individual of the churches are to the likes of Nicodemus, who in the 3rd chapter of John; he lacked the ability to see beyond anything that was of the natural realm.

The anointed "Christ Jesus," was giving him instructions of the spirit. But, it only made since to him that "Jesus" might have been talking to him about doing a natural thing? Which indeed, had already been accomplished in the flesh.

"You must be born again of the spirit." This is the only manner of which an individual can be released from the prison of the flesh, into the realm of the spirit. Nicodemus; discernment of the spirit, was either skewed, or completely turned off! "*In my own opinion.*"

As of late, I am often stumped and disappointed that those who have come to "Christ Jesus," to be saved and set free from the life of sin and of the power of self, they yet need to be informed that there is a much greater purpose and the reason for which they had been saved! Even after they have been saved for a while, dedicated to the local churches.

Honestly, salvation doesn't make since to the newly saved people. Other than the explanation that they will live forever in *"Heaven"* with "God", eternally. What salvation means to them now that they have been saved, is yet to be revealed and or even discovered. It is so much more than just missing the eternal damnation of hell, and the Lake of Fire!

It's no wonder that so many of the younger people in the churches nowadays, feel that being saved is just a waste of time, and a dull boring life. Too many people are encouraged to come down to the altar to be saved, but right afterwards they are handed offering and tithe envelops. They are swiftly introduced to the responsibility of financially supporting the ministry.

People are hardly ever vigorously encouraged to come and to be taught who they are now that they have been saved, and of the powerful authority they now possess as a result. They are strongly invited to become a member of that particular congregation. They are now identified as a church goer, being the only real attribute, which separates them from the lifestyles of living according to the ways of the world.

We are so much more than just members of the local congregations. Being saved and filled with the "Holy Ghost," makes us now citizens of the "Kingdom of God." For which now, we are also citizens of *"Heaven"* already! Although we are still alive and having our natural experience in the earth.

We, can never successfully show ourselves, as true citizens of the "Kingdom of God!" And show forth the spirit and the presences of "God." Until we totally embrace that we are more than just another number on the membership role in the local church. You have got to want so much more than just to have your name called and or recorded in the financial records of the church.

In the churches, we see and we hear a lot of things in the natural and in the spirit. The issue is that while people are indeed seeing and hearing things, they are unable to speak on the experiences, spiritually clarifying them to others. Looking is not the very same as seeing! Often people are looking at things, settling on their own understandings.

While many might pride themselves on their ability to recognize certain characteristics of people, such natural abilities does not constitute discernment. Natural experiences alone can only aid an observant individual to recognize the thing of which they have seen previously. Your mind will always remember indelible impressions made upon you.

WE NEED TO KNOW GOD FIRST

Human intelligence alone of itself, when analytically applied, motivates an individual to mentally ascertain what could be or even what should be the actuality. Through self evaluation and often closer examination of things, a determination of valued self assumptions are obtained.

Detrimentally, people are predestined to absorb what they have believed. People are prone to assign things that might have taken place in the churches, to call them acts of God. Only, there are not always biblical references, to even attest to the fact that it had been wrought in God.

Just because it is called a thing from God, doesn't make it to be so. *And this statement I leave here very cautiously!* At times, the only issue might have been that there was a lack of spiritual discernment. Could have been a move of "God" not very familiar to anything that many of the people present had ever witnessed?

Even when a contradicting relevant fact of truth has been presented, they are already satisfied to keep that of which they had previously ascertained, in their own mind. That of which their minds have retained, they further determine to sustain.

Their findings are substantial for a period of acceptance, avowing to maintain unmovable fixation, even though there had been no proven truth to their own summations. They had found without any evidence from God, that their determination was indeed satisfactory to themselves.

Ascertaining, in ones mind, requires a rigorous mental exploration, to establish what makes since to them. Even if it only makes since to themselves, only! It doesn't matter to them that what they have chosen to embrace in the very spirit of their own minds, just may be disruptive and destructive to their own faithful adherence.

The meaning of the scriptures are often missed by a mile, all based on the assumptions made by people of the churches who have never even been called to preach the word of God. People allow themselves to reinterpret the meaning of the scripture.

They want to hear what suits their since of lack, for convictions of holiness and righteousness and or their feelings at the moment. Many would much rather hear a conforming word to their lifestyles, than to hear a word that requires for them to be transformed.(*Changed*)

On the spiritual side of things, many people are clueless without even realizing they are. They are blinded with their eyes wide open. When the need arises, they are indigent to supply even the more simple solutions to even the most common issues, which plague people on a daily basis.

So as I am building this foundational platform for knowing the difference between the ability to discern and the determination to think that one knows, based on their own reasonable assertiveness. My determination is to establish the necessity to learn to comprehensively flow within the realm of the spirit.

Many invidious debates are made daily about what constitutes hearing the "Voice of "God." The arguments are not even brought concerning whatever He has or hasn't said. The arguments are more-so to the point of trying to determine how, when, and even of where it is, and to whom it is that He speaks to, whenever He might speak.

Most are very adamant in their own belief these days, that "God" doesn't ever speak audibly to man anymore! So how it is that people are determining that "God" is silent, is beyond comprehending. They have already settled in their hearts, that He doesn't even speak? They have even further determined, that the bible itself is likewise silent, for these latter generations.

It is chilling, down in my bones. That people are so sure that the "VOICE AND THE WORD OF GOD" is so outdated! And over exaggerated, relative to speaking to the manner of which people are choosing to live.

So how is it that people are determining to know "God?" When they have erased the very idea of "God" from the forefront of their minds? How do they get to know "God?" When they have come to the conclusion, that the "WORD OF GOD;" (THE BIBLE), is no longer relevant?

People hear the voices of all who have something to say in the media, and in politics. I have witnessed crowds of people as they stopped to listen to an individual speaking on a street corner. No matter what they are sharing and or presenting, they have the attention of the people.

Without "God," there will be no discernment! Without the "WORD OF GOD" and the "HOLY GHOST," there will never be clarity of the scriptures. Spiritual discernment, is of no effort or ability of my own. The "SPIRIT OF GOD" is always going to show us something that we would never see, hear, or to know on our own, without Him.

Of course there are people around the churches, who are seeing things and hearing things about other people. They are in the know about the affairs of the people following the churches, in the community. However, the strength of their so-called knowledge abilities, are all founded upon the arm of the flesh. They get no help from the aid of the spirit!

As a matter of the fact, operating in the realm of the spirit, requires self denial, and much self sacrifice. It is most necessary to give up relying on the will of the flesh, to surrender to being used by the "SPIRIT OF THE LORD." One must learn personally the need for pushing the plate back, while praying and fasting to get into the realm of the spirit.

Those who ascertain in their own minds, are not often given to much prayer. Most people even hardly ever bow their heads during prayer in a public forum, or even at the church. They don't even pray over their food before they eat. Of course it doesn't help that the people praying nowadays over the microphones, are not even spiritually connected to the power of God.

They are praying dead prayers that sink right down to the dirt. Used to be that the prayers prayed during the services at the church were so uplifting. Once the prayer had been prayed, we could go on with the service. Everyone could since the *PRESENCE OF THE "LORD"* in the building, among us.

Our expectations were lifted above our greatest imaginations. Our services were set to the frequencies of getting to know who "God" is! We witnessed what "God" did in the midst of the people in attendance, all because we were made aware of who "God" is! The people in the churches knew when the "PRESENCE OF GOD" had entered into the building.

Used to be that whenever the *PRESENCE OF "GOD"* came into the building, the people silenced their activities, to reverence the PRESENCE OF "LORD." We knew that "God" doesn't show up for no reason at all! It is our responsibility, to acknowledge the PRESENCE OF THE "LORD!" That it may be revealed to us, why it is that "God" has manifested "*HIS PRESENCE,*" at that particular time, in the service.

HEARING HIM, TO KNOW HIM

So many from the leadership platforms, are on guard! To put a stop to the people entering into the PRESENCE OF THE "LORD" during the services! I have heard many of them say to the people of the congregations, you can do all of that at your home. They want the people to sit down and come to order!

Some cannot even detect or since the PRESENCE OF THE "LORD" entering into the service at the church! It is no wonder that they themselves will never be able to discern the meaning nor the messages of *"GOD'S"* SILENCE.

Many people of the churches are totally annoyed at the idea and of the admonishment to hear the "VOICE OF GOD." They don't want to hear the voice of the one who will require for their own lives to change. Conforming them, by the renewing of their minds, to be transformed through the "WRITTEN WORD OF GOD."

While people are resisting the realistic need for hearing the *"VOICE"* and the *"WORD OF GOD,"* they are missing essential facts. Theoretically, written facts that they will never know. Which proves that "God" had never even ceased to speak, through the written word of the bible. People in general, are led to be preoccupied with the hopes, of what "God" can and will do for them!

They are failing to understand, that you can never follow a "God" that you cannot even hear from! Unless "God" speaks back to you, there will never be a dialogue in prayer. As usual, you will do a lot of talking on your knees, but you will not hear Him speak back to you!

"God" so desires, for His people to *"KNOW HIM."* Many people seem to have forgotten that the devil is a deceiver. Satan's deceptions are levied upon people through his VOICE SPEAKING TO THEM. Amazingly, through the examples of your own behavior, you can hear the devil's suggestions to you, to cause you to do wrong!

But, you can't hear the VOICE OF THE "LORD" calling you, to live righteously in holiness! Through the *"WORD OF GOD,"* you will come to know, that you alone of yourselves, are no match for the devil.

The satanic voice have already caused a separation and eternal disaster in the role of humanity. The master deceiver already know how to cause you trouble and how to dull your hearing and the desire to ever hear the *"Voice of God."*

Satan even knows, that to hear "God;" is to know "God!" This is how he knows that he is the devil, doomed for eternal destruction. He has heard the *"Voice of God"* tell him that he is no longer worthy, nor welcome to worship "God!"

It is too important to know the *"Voice of God."* We should at all times, practice the presence of "God!" In effort to know the "voice" and the "spirit of God," in the fullness of His power. We need to hear Him speaking to us, approving of our worship and praise to Him.

"God" is seated on the throne, ever watching over the people of the earth, attuned unto our prayers. "God" knows those of us who are indeed His! He knows who have been washed in the *"Blood of Jesus Christ,"* transformed by the renewing of our minds. "God;" knows those of us that have given our ear to Him, through the *"word of God."*

I am of the opinion; that the primary reasons that people are totally knocked off, whenever *"God is silent,"* is for the reason of the fact that they had not prepared themselves to know the ways of "God," through the *"Word of God."* They have never been taught or have never learned to listen for the "voice of God."

They are not flexible in their spirit, mind, soul, and bodies to follow "God," as He speaks to them on a daily basis. People have not been made obedient to any command of "God." Which would say to them, to just wait on the "Lord" until He speaks again! Romans 8:14;

Most people for sure have never learned to be patient with "God," they never learned to wait! "God" moves at the His own will and discretion. Of the more minute things that "God" knows, when to speak would definitely be one of those things.

"God" is so worth waiting for! You will never regret that you waited on the "Lord!" Often, as we wait on the "Lord," things appear to be greatly magnified, even more than they really are. As "God" begins to work those things out for us, we begin to see and to realize, just how small and tiny those things were to the "*WILL*" and to the "*POWER OF GOD.*"

"God" never requires for us to wait on Him for any reasons that would suggest that he is angry or disapproving of what we have asked of Him. His Love is so much greater than that!

"GOD'S SILENCE," is much greater than your need to hear Him speaking to your need or to your request. The message of "GOD'S SILENCE" is more powerful than the enemy's onslaught against you! Whenever "God" chooses not to speak, it is to be understood that the POWER and the STRENGTH of "God's" voice, could mean the very end of things for you. So just listen and wait!

"God" knows why it is best for Him not to speak to you or even for you. He knows when you have not regarded what He has already said to you in the "*WRITTEN WORD OF GOD!*" "God" is not at all slipping concerning you and your refusal to do and to be what He has commanded of you, in the "WORD OF GOD."

"God" has been waiting on you, to hear from you in prayer, and you are yet keeping Him on hold! You've been silent for a very long time! How is it that you have not made the same issue with that fact, that you have made concerning "*GOD'S SILENCE?*"

You think that you can let yourselves off the hook, while you hold "God" accountable, for saying nothing concerning you! Somehow, you allow yourselves to believe, that your silence to "God" punishes Him, or even saddens Him? Con-

Discerning God's Silence

sider the fact; that there are too many people that do talk to and with "God," on a daily basis.

"God," is not suffering the need of any communication or of a conversation. Every living thing on the entire face of the planet earth, have their conversations with "God!" The ground and the seeds which are planted into the ground talk with "God." The creeping crawling things, talk with "God."

The leaves on the trees, talk with "God." All of the plant life, talk with the "Father!" His is the maker and the creator of all things. As a human being, a person, you need definitely to talk with "God". There is nothing that our "God" cannot hear, nor understand!

Discernment, enables us to not only know the difference between the "*Voice of "God*" from the voice of the enemy! It aids us in being able to comprehend the need for patiently waiting on the "Lord" in the times of our needs.

The gift of discernment flows better and even greater as we grow and mature in the "Lord." Once we have had an experience with the "Lord," we will never forget the emotional lows or the discouragement that we might have felt. However, we will likewise never forget the powerful response and actions of His angelic defense, to rescue us.

So many benefits have been given to those of us who have been transformed into the "Kingdom of God's Dear Son." Many can confuse being greedy with the boldness to freely ask for whatever it may be that we need from the "Father," at any time! It is our given privilege, to receive from the hand of our "Father," every time that He purposes to give unto us!

We mature to actuate the exactness of our relativity to the things of the spirit, through discernment! We will no longer find ourselves, saying, that *something told us* to do a certain thing. Now, we are more adaptable to be heard saying the "*spirit of the Lord*" led me to do!

Now that we will have learned to discern the "*voice of*

"God" telling us to do or to say any certain thing, we are also more assuredly capable of discerning the absence of the *"Voice of God."* He is silent not by accident, or by happenstance, but, by divine providence! "God" is intentional!

No instruction is given, and neither is there a word spoken to show us anything at all. As there is nothing or no one in the earth's atmosphere that can stop "God" from speaking, you might as well accept His Silence!

"God's Silence," is powerful, isn't it!!!

Chapter 5

The Unrestricted Lord

For the word of God is quick and powerful, and sharper than any twoedged sword, piercing even to the dividing asunder of soul and spirit, and of the joints and marrow, and is a discerner of the thoughts and intents of the heart. Neither is there any other creature that is not manifest in His sight: but all things are naked and open unto the eyes of him with whom we have to do. Seeing then that we have a great high priest, that is passed into the heavens, Jesus the son of God, let us hold fast our profession. For we have not an high priest which cannot be touched with the feeling of our infirmities: but was in all points tempted like as are we, yet without sin. Let us therefore come boldly before the throne of grace, that we may obtain mercy and find grace to help in the time of need. HEBREWS 4:12-16;

THE HIGHEST, MOST QUALIFIED, HEAR HIM

I am quite moved to the core, saddened for everyone who may have decided against believing, trusting and having a relationship with God; in Christ Jesus; The Holy Ghost. People, no matter what you may have been led to believe, we need the Lord in our lives. Whenever God does speak we need desperately to hear what He says.

There is no one else anywhere that could ever love you

and care for you in this life, while preparing for you to live forever in Heave with Him. Such disdain for God had been bred and developed over the process of time, simply because it had been discovered that God will answer to no one!

It is so fascinating to me that God doesn't have to give an account about where He's been or of wherever He is. God being omnipresent, means that He is all over the place, everywhere, at all times, but simultaneously, at the same time. If there were any other place to go other than to be everywhere that He already is, perhaps God would either go there or He'd already be there too!

God made everywhere that there is to be, no place is obscure to Him. There is no such place to be called as nowhere, or null and void to Him! Understand it like this, "EVERYWHERE" ~ is already in God from the beginning! In turn there is never a challenge for God to be anywhere. God is everywhere He desires to be, with the exception to the hearts and the minds of all people who yet fail to let Him in.

Perhaps you are one of the many people who have determined in your heart that it would better serve you if God were absent from all of the business affairs of your lives? I suggest that you had better find another earth or a world that doesn't belong to God. Wherever you are and everywhere that you may desire to either go or to be, God is already there!

You might want to consider that God has already been everywhere that we most likely will never be privileged to go, in our lifetime. The absolute only place that you could ever be successful at keeping God out of is your own heart! He, even though uninvited by you, passes through many fleeting thoughts in your mind everyday, when you never purposefully intended for Him to. At no effort of your own, you can't stop Him!

Whenever you least expect the thought of Jesus Christ, there it comes flowing through your thoughts. Many swiftly pass it on through to avoid it from filtering through the thought process of their thinking. Others may think on it momentarily, while some are captured and whisked away with the very thought of the awesomeness of Christ.

Somewhere, someplace, and at some unsuspected times, the name of the Lord is either spoken, written on an advertisement, or even seen on a television screen. Many people across the social media platforms say the name of Jesus Christ. Music that mentions the name of Jesus Christ is often heard playing.

Either way, He has walked through the minds of many, though the doors of their hearts have been kept securely shut. There is no denying that He has been through your mind, while there just may be undeniable evidence the He has never entered into your heart.

God's been to the bottom of the ocean and the sea, have you been there? He's been to the ceiling of the skies and of space, have you been there? He's been to the depths of hell, to the very bottom of the bottomless pit, have you been there? Everywhere forbidden for all of mankind to go, God's been there too. But have you been there?

Many people are angry with God's decisions because they would prefer that He might consider them first and ask for their permission to be the awesomely powerful God that He indeed is! If God had to have our permission for anything, He wouldn't be God! While He does prefer to be in agreement with us, He is not asking for us to allow for Him to be who He Is; as He; Is! In Heaven and in all of the earth!

Inferior ~~gods~~ of No Comparison

Since back to the very beginning of time, people wanted a god that they could control and tell them what to do for them when they wanted them to. Amazingly, the other gods chosen by the people were formed and fashioned of their own mannish desires. They made them from the material

The Sovereignty of God's Silence

substances from the creator, that were found in the earth.

They used metals, wood, stone, and other material substances. They made gods that they could never also give a spirit and power. They were as dead as the materials that they were formed of. They had ears, but they could not hear them praying to them. They gave them eyes but they could not see them. They even gave them hands that could never touch them or give help to them.

They sort of inadvertently depended on God to help them build their gods, though ignorantly blinded and totally deceived! Foolishly, they used God's creative awesomeness against Him, without trying to do so! God created all of the material substances that were later used to fashion the other gods that they chose to bow down to, for prayer, praise, and for worship.

I will say to you, that if you're that mad and angry with God, get your hands off of all His stuff. Get your feet off of His earth! How about closing your eyes to His brilliant light of the day and of the night. Try hiding yourselves from the sunlight, or from the openness of the air. Try finding other air to breathe which doesn't come from the Lord.

Try living on forever, defying the sentence of death passed on to all mankind, never dying in the earth. You did not create your own blood, try giving it back to God who gave it to you from the beginning. Since it is your choice to do whatever you want to do with your body, since you're so mad at God for giving you that body, won't you just give it back to Him! Literally! Give it back!

"[*I DID NOT SAY, NEITHER DID I MEAN TO SAY FOR YOU TO COMMIT SUICIDE!*]"

You will never be able to change nor to alter who God is! Rejecting God doesn't have any kind of an effect on Him being God! If you understood the essence and the eternal timeless characteristics of God, you'd understand that God have no time to become someone else. He has no choice of being any other being, other than who He already Is! God is neither a creature or of any habit of time. Time have no bearing on the existing presence of God. God owns time! Time is controlled by God! Time belongs to God!

God Is In Charge of Now

Time came on the scene and into existence for us as mankind in the earth. But, it came about way too late to have had any effecting alterations on the reality, and of the person of God! Time itself, didn't just happen all of it's own strength and power. Time needed God to exist, so it had to wait in line for God to call it's name to come forth to begin to click. All of the elements of time were held hostage to the will and to the word of God.

Time lulled immobilely paralyzed, folded away as the awaiting blanket to rhythmically adorn the existence of the tick - tock in the clock. Until God gave the word for time to begin to spread and to count. Everything moves in time but with the rhythmic cadence of time. Just where would the beat of the cadence be without the measurement of time.

There is no movement of the sound in music to change the necessary voicing of the notation of chords, without the command of time. As the music conductor waves their wand over the orchestra, it bears no meaning at all without the commanding rhythm of time.

Time always measures the necessity for the period of change for all of humanity. With every move that we make, it is also paramount to know of the time limit, or of the time span alloted to make that move.

Time is of the greatest importance to us in the earth. Not even the sun is allowed to shine on us always, around the clock. As there is a limit for the day as well as for the night. No man on the face of the earth have the ability to speak to the sun to the keeping of the scheduled assignment, to shine on the earth. The moon equally has its alloted time to give it's light to the night. Time speaks to us and for us all!

Have you ever stopped to ask yourselves, where was time before it was actually begun? Do you think that time had any idea that all of the things of the earth would exist inside of it?

Time had no heartbeat, or a metronome to measure when to begin or to end, or for even determining how long it will be or had been! God knew that man would eventually use the measurement of time for working, worshiping, fasting and praying. Time would eventually be used for governing the speed for which we could travel to and from a certain distance.

All that has come with time and in the precesses of time, all came at the command of God. Things as we know of them today were held in cue until God gave the consent for them to leap into existence. Time follows after the power and the presence of God, as time needs God. Time will run out for sure in the presence of God.

Whenever time ceases to exist, God will be as He has always been, who He Is! Time has been ancient and old, it has been new and young. Time have been said to move slowly, while others have complained that the time moved way too fast! Yet, in the face of swiftly moving time, God is just the same as He always is, and will always be!

Now; ticks onwards as it adorns the present countenance on the face of time with every secondary movement of the second hand on the clock. Now is sooner than ever expected to swiftly pass on by to become then, back when. Now; as the existing reality that it is, have been given the command to swiftly fade away much quicker and faster than a vapor of steam.

As prevalent and as precious as the time of now is, even right now; it is not patient, neither respectful to wait for any of us to be there with it as it shows up. Now will come and go, with or without you! Now leaves us without notice or even without show of a sign of any kind, not even a trace. We are restricted to be here right in place when now shows up for us, else we soon are left to wonder where the time went.

GOD; ALL BY HIMSELF

Unlike us as mankind, God have the power to arrest that which we know of as the "NOW!" Causing it to stay in place remaining until His will and plans for us is accomplished. God says when **NOW** can be the exact planned space of claim, according as He wills for it to be for us, whereas we could recognize it as the RIGHT(exact), NOW!

Supposed time were to stand still, unmovable for an immeasurable span of timeless existence, whereas right now as we know of it, would always remain to be right now? Would it be enough for us in the earth to recognize it as being God's silence?

If everything stopped moving as the movement of time seized throughout the earth, with exception to mankind, what would we be willing to think? Would we think that God had become silent, or would we recognize that He had been that way for quite some time now?

Of course many scientific thinkers would be more willing to think that something had gone wrong in the makeup of God. Mere men of carnal secular thinking, are prone to hold God accountable for everything that cease to function as it was previously designed to do. I doubt that the idea of God being in control of everything, would be shown any or of much mercy at all!

It is appalling to see people shake their fist at the sky while they use profanity and swear at the name of Jesus Christ. The simple antics and the spoiled childlike behavior of mankind don't rattle the peace and the presence of God. You can imagine just about how much of that behavior might be taking place at such a crisis to humanity. While people will spin out of control at will, God is always in control.

Disobedient people who will never do what God has asked of them to do, they throw tantrums and have fits of rage whenever God does what they never wanted Him to do! Somehow they overlook or simply dismiss that fact that God remains to be who He is, even in spite of who they remain to be.

No matter what God chooses to do, when He chooses to do it, and or to whom He has chosen to do it to, He's always righteous and correct. As much as I simply love referring to the beginning, I am hard pressed to deal with the reality of God with us in the present.

So many people are satisfied to acknowledge God of the past ages. They'd like to believe that God doesn't even exist anymore. Somehow they have been convinced that God just may have created and even started everything as we know of it today. Foolishly, they have allowed for themselves to settle their minds to believe that God finished His work and left it here to the will and the discretion of man in the earth to do whatever we as mankind will choose to do with it.

In my own heart, mind, soul and spirit, based on my observation of the things that no man could have ever been responsible for, I know that it's a fact that God is alive and quite well! The beauty and the splendor of the things created are awe striking, even at a glance. The very fact that all living creatures live and breathe, eat and sleep, and even create after their own kind, is all God's plan.

The intelligence of plant life, is mind boggling, stirring the botanical interest of mankind all across the globe of the earth. They'd like to have an in depth knowledge base of just what causes all plants to thrive. People are left with no choice but to explore to determine whether they can make

Unrestricted Lord

any since of life and the living ability of plants. In the sea, plants are more alive than at first they were thought to be.

Scientist in the laboratories have gone as far as to split the genus of the seeds in the plants, to cross genetically compound the germination of the seeds. Somehow they were not satisfied to accept that God made everything just the way that He wanted things to be. Even though they may have been successful to cross produce plants, the innate nature of the plants for reaching upwards could never be altered.

We see trees, vines, and even shrubbery latch on to one another, growing upwards towards the sky. Have you taken the time to notice that all plant life reach upwards towards the sky? What man could have been swift enough to move about the entire planet to instruct plant life to reach for the light of the sun?

It is only because of God that we know of the differences between the tops and the bottoms. In the earth among people of all origins, it is ingrained within our natural intelligence to not only know what is the top, but also to know that we must reach upwards to touch the top. Although the tops of so many things are unreachable for us in the earth, never is there ever realized that the tops are now removed to rest on the bottom!

All tops are upwards located above the common norm among us in the earth. Most everyone in life are reaching for the top in every aspect of living. Whether it is realized that we may have to climb, hiking our way up the mountain side, drive up the hillside in the direction of the north, or to travel there by way of aircraft? Either way, we know that we are determined to go upwards.

Heights are established and further determined by God. Else there would not have been a reason for the wings of birds and all of the foul of the air. Wings were given not only for the flying animals of creation to soar through the heights, but also for the ability to lift themselves to perch and to roost in the tops of the trees where most land predators could never reach them.

Many of the tree tops are elevated high in to the sky above the land and the sea. Nevertheless, God has given wisdom to certain species to build their abodes among the branches in the tops of the same trees. It is bewildering to most mankind, that the mountain which are made of rocks most powerful affixed to the earth and beneath sea floor, they are also given to reach upwards, even into the clouds of the sky.

Certain species of the earth were given hooves to climb the rocks, sure footed at an instance. As high as the mountains are and as thin as the air up there is, making it almost impossible for most men to breathe there, certain species of the animal kingdom are found living there. Upwards come from the all omnipotent God, who has also given the established purpose for it.

We know for sure the difference in the head from that of the foot. We also know the difference from the head and the tail. It takes but only slight intelligence to see and to recognize the positioning of the head of all mankind and the positioning of the heads of all animals and fish in the sea.

The truthful relevance had been established for us in the earth since from the beginning of creation. The head of man is located at the top of the body, so as to keep us continually head-wards to Heaven. From the top of our heads to the souls of our feet, we belong to God! We understand that up is where God is indeed! God planned that man and God would ever be in communication. Therefore, our heads are upwards attuned to the frequency to the spirit of God.

All that we as the people of the earth would ever need to communicate with God, are first created in the head. The paralleled polarity of truth in the spirit realm and in the natural realm, are located at the head of mankind. God intended that we know Him for just who He is! Our brains and our minds are located in the head!

It is furthermore most necessary that we as mankind learn to hear the voice of God speaking to us. God plans for us to see Him through His written word. Thus, we also develop the love for speaking His name as we learn to pray to Him, worshiping Him in the beauty of His holiness. Through the spirit of God we soon Taste of the spirit of God. We taste and see that the Lord is good!

We see what God does for us all of the time, but it is paramount that we are to become knowledgeable of who God Is! We are equipped with the tools for being able to hear God speaking to us in the earth. However, sin and iniquity have clogged up the head!

The head of mankind is yet still where God created it to be, but the mind and the spirit of man are in a sunken state of wickedness. There can be no communication with God in such a state. Repentance is much needed!

CHAPTER 6

God; Treads Above Sound

For God has not given us the spirit of fear But of power, and of love and of a sound mind.
II Timothy 1:7

Comprehending the Meaning of Sound

As we begin this particular topic of discussion, it is very important that we garner understanding, so that the definition of sound can be more deeply absorbed. One dimensional ideology of reasoning, can no longer be sufficient, for wrapping our minds around the complete meaningful scope of knowledge, relative to the structured relevance in the language usage of the word, sound.

The word *"SOUND"* in and of itself, in definition, does not always give reference only to a generated factor of noise! Sound or noise generators are more so purposed to establish direct pin-pointed intention of recognition. There is no way at all to be of soundness in mind ,of soul, or of spirit without intended efforts to cause such soundness to be realized.

I endeavor to not only give reference to the audible sound waves created, but to also give recognition to the factors which make the noise. In many instances of greater relevance, of which will be the depths of my discussion, is the need to know. *TO BE "SOUND" ~ MEANS TO BE STABLE, AND OR TO BE ASSURED, SECURELY AFFIXED TO THE SURFACE OF SOMETHING, IT IS CONCRETELY SOLIDIFIED.*

That which is *SOUND IS ALSO INDICATIVE OF MEANING THAT*

IT IS ACCURATE AND FLAWLESS OF PRESENT UNDERSTANDING OF A FACT, A THEORY, A DEFINITIVE MEANING IN A WORD OR PHRASE ETC. Unfounded ideas, are never productive of soundness in the minds and the heart of an individual. Many are encouraged to allow fleeting thoughts, and run away conditions of their minds, whereas their thinking is swiftly canceled, concerning everything, through questioning.

Issues or questions which require a more extensive search for a definitive comprehension, which is the direct resulting products of wandering minds, can't be presently viewed as being fundamentally sound. Although inquiry minds want to know, over-thinking and ultimately questioning every minute detail of most everything, leads to the breakdown and the dismantling of deliberate intentional soundness.

Often, many people are yet in the midst of their search never haven found that of which they have been seeking. It has also become a fact of knowledge that they can never be satisfied, for the simple reason of questioning everything, but believing absolutely nothing. Their minds eye has become blinded, disallowing a mental grasp to the find of their search.

Such people can never be resolute in theory or in doctrinal aspects of faith and truth. They spend the balance of their time trying to get over to the other side, or possibly to the underside of facts and of theories. That of which definitively settles the matter, is too often passed over as a matter of the fact resolution. There just has to be more to be explored and possibly found; they might think?

There is absolutely nothing wrong with seeking greater knowledge and understanding. But to what extent are you willing to go about seeking, when faced with a sound, infallible, unwavering truth, as the word of God is indeed? Complete soundness of truth and of reasoning have been laid out before you, but it is of no consequence to those who refuse to accept it! Deliberate searching continuously, even after a find, most often may be indicative of the outright refusal to believe that what has indeed been revealed is the answer and the right find to what has been sought after.

I am of the opinion that much of today's leadership of the churches, that they are not at all of sound minds and thinking, as it relates to the *WRITTEN WORD OF "GOD."* Many are most certainly not biblically sound in their teaching, they don't really seem to adhere to the written report of the scriptures.

They are now too interested and taken with the ideas of finding ways to skirt around the truth! So as, to allow for the people in the churches to avoid head on collisions with the truth, which contradicts their chosen lifestyles! Going on, heart forward, and growing into uprighted stable disciples of faith in *"CHRIST JESUS,"* is not going to be clearly witnessed should this type of leadership continues to lead the flock astray.

That which should indeed be received as sound teaching in the churches, is that to which the people being taught will be able to follow as infallible guides to rely on at any time, when needed. They're at the church, but not in the church! They still want to do whatever they choose to do in the world, regardless to what the word of God has to say about it. They are neither settled or affixed to the will and to the plan of God for their own lives.

Amazingly, the same people that are listening for a sound from the Lord, they are not even sound in faith or the word of God. They are not interested in learning and being taught to hear the soundness of the spirit of the Lord through the word of God. Those that want to remain a part of the activities of the world, they should just go ahead and stay out there in the world. *A bit of soundness for your mind!*

We need most definitely to be sound in every aspect of our being. So many people are seeking someone else to blame for the horrific details of their lives, as result of their own bad decisions. People want to be respected and to be esteemed people of great integrity. They are demanding of such recognition, but all the while they are perpetually displaying that they are unstable everywhere you look at them!

Soundness of mind, soul, and of the spirit will be the defining factors later on, which allows for making more significant decisions. Soundness, will be worn as a badge of honor on the shoulder of your garment. The same manner of which an officer of the United States Armed Forces is saluted and respected, those who come into contact with you will also find it plausible to show you the like favor of your earned reverential esteem.

In the exacting of the writing of a will, it is always thought to be carried out by persons of a sound mind. Doesn't really matter who an attorney might have been, if the person could not have written the will on their own recognizance, it is considered to be null and void! Even in a hospital, a sick patient can only make decisions if they are of a sound mind! Else, otherwise, it is required that they have a person with the power of attorney.

Many are not really respectful to the necessity of having a sound mind. They are fallen into the idea of not taking life too seriously. Only when it is necessary to be about our most extreme wits, many are found to be in animated states of recreation thinking. Even while on their work schedules, figuratively speaking, they are mentally on vacation. Not much is ever really taken seriously by them.

In our judicial systems, witnesses and criminal defendants are examined to establish whether they are credible sound persons, to withstand the scrutiny on the witness stand during court precedings. Those who are not found to be sound of mind, can not be trusted to make statements which may bear life altering results to the future status, in the lives of others.

Certain very important testimonies and evidence have been rejected and thrown out of the case files, as result of the insecure manner of which they might have been acquired. Law professionals in the judicial system, from the investigating officers, all of the way up to the judge, are required to be sure that the criminal suspect or any witnesses, that they are sound of their own minds.

Creative Sound in Noise Making

All that is "*AUDIO*"~*meaning noise vibrations in the production of sound creations,* began as "God" began to create. The production of all that is audible was all for the sake of distinct discernment while hearing. All of creation have been given the uniqueness of individuality, whereas no two things or people were intended to sound exactly alike.

Imagine the orchestra having so many different instruments. It is so important that every instrument play its own part. Supposed every instrument sounded exactly alike? That scenario is not one that is easily imagined! Now just what kind of noise do you think that would be? By the way of its own originated sound, God has made it more easily attainable for everything on the planet earth to say its own name.

Sound origination separates the distinction for calling up any intended creature or created thing dwelling in the earth. "God" gave every created being in the earth its own voice/sound stamp. These audio certainties have lasted and they will last throughout all of creation. Of course we could all imagine the confusion and even the danger should a brute beast approach one us sounding as if it were a tiny bird!

Most things in this life are identifiable to us as result of visual aid. We recognize what we are seeing based on its own unique dress and body build. However even in the distance we might just be able to distinguish a creature through the aid of the sound of its mouth. Many different sounds come from the mouths of the animals of the earth.

The command of sound comes from the "Lord" above. As "God" *IS NOT THE AUTHOR OF CONFUSION*, it has been given for us to know things and people alike, without error. There are sounds that we are very knowledgeably familiar to recognize. There are yet other unknown sounds that causes us much unrest. Most of the sounds in the earth are commonly discerned by us.

Through the many years of our existence upon the earth we have become quite familiar to the everyday sounds of the earth. Many people are gifted to discern the diverse unique sounds, without needing to visualize them. They have very photostatic memories which have made an indelible audio imprint of the sounds in their memory.

Lots of people are traumatized at the sound of the thunder as it roars across the sky. While watching the gathering of the dark clouds giving indication of the coming storms. Most of us, sort of set ourselves for the greatly swollen claps of thunder. Since our childhood, we have come to understand that the thunder up above us in the sky, is sending us the message to prepare ourselves for what just might be torrential downpours.

It had been most common that people would pay attention and even give respect to the messages of the sky. People would close the windows and shut the doors. They would bring in their plants and often even bring their pets in out of the storms. It was just normal for people to take precaution to the eminent threatening sound of the coming storm.

As result of the greater howling of the wind blowing across the earth and the sky, the more we knew that the greater plans for protecting ourselves should be seriously engaged, immediately. "God" has always sent the messages of warning before the destruction. It is more common of these latter times that people are more so determined to test the power of the storm threats.

Many lives have been taken and destroyed as result of ignoring the signs of the coming destruction. We have witnessed the weather disasters through the news medias. People are rather influenced to believe that the news and the weather reports are all fake and unrealistic.

They think that they are naturally warranted the right to stay the course to see if there just might be the chance to outweigh the report of the weather. As a result, people have been washed away in the storm disaster, out to sea, or somewhere they will never be seen again.

This rather rebellious, stubborn generation of people nowadays, are often found trying to "*BUILD STORM SHELTERS, RIGHT IN THE MIDDLE OF THE STORMS.*" It is not at all sound thinking to procrastinate in the presence of such severe warnings. "God" loves us way too much to allow for us to stand in the judgment trying to say that we never knew!

You just might be further led to believe that "God" indeed is silent, believing that He has allowed for the gay communities to taker over and to distort the originated meaning of the *RAINBOW SIGN* across the sky? "God" told "*NOAH*" after the flood had ended, that there would be no more WATER to destroy the earth, but FIRE next time!

Many people never even knew that the word gay was originally used to describe happy people. The devil will always show you a little good, in order to feed you a whole lot of bad! It appear that we are seeing the rainbow across the sky just as beautiful as it has always been, more than usually! The gay agenda refuses to adhere to the warning sign of the rainbow instead.

It doesn't take a rocket science to see and to witness that the rainbow shows up after very heavy rain falls and storms. We are often assured that rain is stopping for a while! The rain stops just as it has been required to do from the beginning. This is no time for the party to get restarted! It is though, the great reminder of the fact that "God" has promised to have something much more devastating and permanently destructive for the earth! For the corruption and for all of the people who play their part in bringing the corruption to the lives of the other people.

NOTE: ~ Every time that you see the rainbow across the sky, you need to hear the message that "God" is sending to us in the earth, through the awesome sight that you are seeing! *"FIRE IS COMING SOON!"*

Could you ever imagine the many people who were lost as result of weather disasters and other earth disasters, who would not adhere to the warnings to take cover, or either to remove themselves from the endangered area of warning? Perhaps they think that they just may get the opportunity to argue with "God," suggesting that their demise was so unfair?

It is very sound indeed, if you would go ahead and check yourselves to be assured that you are prepared for the eminent coming of the Lord! It is even better for you to prepare yourselves for death should the Lord delay His coming!

Have You Heard, God's Coming Through

Since the departure of our *"LORD JESUS CHRIST,"* we were informed that the same way of which He left us, He's coming back again.[Acts 1:11] Haven't you heard this report before? Are you one of those people who are determined to believe that this is all just a bunch of junk?

See, I know that it is so much easier to live unsure while living as a sinner in this sin riddled world. Assurance is required for all of those of us who live by faith. All must be sound in our minds, so as to knowing that we are in the faith that pleases "God" and keeps us soundly affixed to the GOSPEL OF THE *"KINGDOM OF GOD!"*

I have met with so many people who were either ashamed or totally unsure, as it relates to *"THE FAITH OF JESUS CHRIST."*

I have been called to pray for many sick people who had never embraced any faith in "God". They wanted "God" to heal them and allow for their lives to continue on, but they never wanted "Christ Jesus" to be the savior of their souls.

Perhaps it just might be beneficial to know that "God" doesn't heal anyone that He can't have as result! The book of "James;" tells us that when the elders of the churches are call to pray for the sick, that if there be any sins they shall be forgiven. "God" doesn't forgive us for the greater benefit of Satan, for self, or for sin and iniquity!

Even before "God" comes back to receive the church out of this world, He's coming through in the spirit for you. He's coming through with a final warning, with healing, with deliverance to free you from the power of sin and iniquity! Or maybe just to comfort you, through the pain of grief from losing someone in death who was indeed dear to your heart.

He coming to tread down upon all of things that we are being plagued and or tormented with. When He comes my friend, He is not intending to leave things as they are whenever He came to you. Maybe you're thinking that *He is silent* because He hasn't gotten there to you as of yet? Check yourselves! Have you even asked for Him to come for you? "James;" says; "*that you have not because you ask not...*"

Just how highly are you exalted on the throne of your own selves. "God" will have no other gods before Him, and He doesn't apologize. You can't love yourselves more than you love "God," and expect for Him to come through for you! "God" is not begging and pleading for someone to allow for Him to show Himself strong and mighty. It should be known of the entire planet earth of just how mighty and powerful *"GOD IS!"*

Go ahead and put you minds to rest to stop thinking that "God" is in need of you! We are totally in need of "God!" "God" says in the scripture, "*if I were hungry I would not tell you!"* You go and look that up in the "KJV" of the holy bible, for yourselves!

There are aspects of which "God" does need us as people in the earth aligned with. For and instance, "God" needs for us to stand in faith believing that He is going to do just what He said He would do. "God" needs for us to trust Him without a doubt. "God" needs for us to embrace the written word of God, for the sake of the "Kingdom Of God."

"God" needs for us, to be living examples and en-samples of the goodness and of *"the grace of God."* With all of the sound that is created while we worship and praise the "Lord," the sounds that we make are to become the entry way for the "Lord" to tread upon our awareness of His presence.

"God" so wisely treads upon our atmospheres, so as not to crush us under the power of His steps. He treads above sound for the purpose of keeping us in tune to the fact that *"He is God all by Himself!"* We will never be given the right to believe that "God" could not have worked on our behalf without our assistance or our guidance.

"God" is always above the earth and above all of mankind. We are not at eye level with "God." While we are required to seek the face of "God," it is to be better understood that we are not even worthy to come face to face with "God," as we live on the earth. All will see Him just as He is, when He comes back to receive us out of the world.

If you can recall, "God" said to Moses on Mt. Sinai; **"No man has ever seen God face to face and lived!"** "God" forever treads above the total soundness of all mankind. For this reason alone, "God" hates pride! Pride suggests to us that we just may be able to stand with "God" on the very same platform as He is! Pride lies to mankind all of the time! We can never know "God" in the fullness of His power in pride.

Those who are in pride on a daily basis, they are the very same ones who are so disturbed whenever they have finally decided that "God" should talk to them, but He doesn't! Pride will have you to believed that all of Heaven should know who you are, you might be led to think.

You have lost all sobriety of your mind, if you think for one moment that "God" has to bow to your place of status in the earth. Pride will not even allow for you to realize that your authority is limited to only a small portion of the earth. Not everyone is even required to respect your authority and power on the face of the planet.

Those of who have amassed great wealth and financial acuity, are soon brought to the greater reality that they are not the only persons of the earth with great financial status. Someone else had the riches before you were even born to the earth! Your numbers are never greater than "God's!"

Many of the riches people of the earth are fearful of being betrayed by other people of all origins. "God" is never threatened or concerned with being betrayed, not even by you! "God's" numbers are forever secured. "God;" is secured with being "God;" as my brother and good friend and fellow laborer of the gospel, "A*POSTLE* M*ICHAEL* F*ANTROY*" always says; "A*IN'T NOBODY* G*OD, BUT* G*OD!*"

"God" never fails; He doesn't bear any flaws; He's too perfect to ever make any mistakes! He sees and He knows everything that there is to know about everything that there is to be known! "F*ROM EVERLASTING TO EVERLASTING,* G*OD* I*S* G*OD!*"

S*OUNDNESS*, is not a thing that "God" has to ever worry about being, or maintaining. "God's" got His foot on all that is sound indeed, therefore He knows all of who are indeed sound all over the face of the earth. Even as He knows the distinction of every audible sound in the earth, He know the soundness of every person, and of every sound decision.

"G*OD*" *LOVES SOUNDNESS!* He is not often seen or viewed as being silent to those who are indeed sound of mind, soul, and of their spirit. The older generations used to sing a song which said, *"Keep Your Lamps Trimmed and Burning!"* I've matured to realize that they were talking about us keeping our minds sober and sound before the "Lord."

My advise to you is; *"Don't make a Sound, Until you are Sound within your own selves!"* Can you hear Him Now?

Chapter 7

Disdained God's Order

Behold, the Lord's hand is not shortened, that it cannot save; neither his ear heavy that it cannot hear; but your iniquities have separated between you and your God, and your sins have hid his face from you, that he will not hear. Isaiah 59:1-2; *And Because iniquity shall abound, the love of many shall wax cold.* Matthew 24:12;

Let The People of The Church Come To Order

There is so much confusion among the churches all across the land. Doesn't appear to matter how wrong they each have become, they all are yet determined to confess that they belong to God. There seems to be no more power of the presence of God in the churches. The people are gone wild right in the aisle of the sanctuaries.

The love of God is yet as powerfully sound and intact, as it has always been. It's the lack of love from the people at the churches which have grown cold. Many people of the churches would pull out their bill folds and wallets to aid another person in need. They pull out their cell phones now to go viral filming the persons in need of the assistance from the church.

Coming to the aid of the people of the community is all a great big joke, or just another let me show you what my church can do, video; for social media. The churches don't mind doing food drives and clothing give aways, just as long as they can have the attention of the media. People are hungry everyday of their lives. Their children are in need of daily nourishment to help them to focus and to learn while in class at school.

Many of today's leaders have downright forgotten that they used to be the disobedient children from the past, in their own childhood. Some of the other members of the church and of their communities helped their parents, and kept them straight when they were away from their homes.

Now the pastors, many of them anyway, are too busy preparing for television ministries and talk shows. They have more important agendas which require the greater balance of their time now. We often hear of the problems that plague the youth of today. Rarely are we hearing of the churches being part of the solution to get the young people back on track.

Most of the churches say that they want to hear from the Lord! While one church is black balling another church to their congregation. Preachers are fighting against other preachers; men are against the women; the women are likewise against the men of the churches. The adults are fighting against the youth, the youth are rebelling against the leaders of the churches, and the teachings of holiness and of truth.

Leadership have softened the requirement for the dress code in the churches. People will go everywhere in uniform with exception to the church. Whatever their jobs are requiring for them to wear, they dare not show up there in regular street clothing. Used to be that everybody had their own Sunday best cloths to wear to church.

The meaning of it all got lost in translation as the people complained about the dress requirement in the churches. They have taken the "COME AS YOU ARE," meaning way to far to the left outside of the scripture. Without even knowing it, they are saying to the leadership nowadays; *"but we never really wanted to change anyway."* Let us dress the way that we want to, God know our hearts.

It is true that God does know your hearts, however He is requiring the leaders of the churches to go and to make disciples of men, or of people. It's not easy to make disciples when the people of the churches are out of order, on purpose!

A DISCIPLE ~ *"is a disciplined learner."* Where is the discipline in rejection, adamant resistance to the teachings of the churches. Where is the example of discipline when even the pastor dresses in the pulpit, just like they just left the neighborhood park, with all of the *homies?*

Whenever you, as a member of the church, sit around in discussions with the other people who are not yet members of the church, and talk negatively about the church, you just may be causing the unsaved people to stay away from very place to find "God," for the saving of their souls!

We are seeing more discipline breakers than we are seeing disciple makers. Many people who have been at the church for many years but have never surrendered to the "WORD OF GOD," nor to the leadership, they call themselves being angry with "THE WORD OF GOD." The "WORD OF GOD," doesn't change for any of us in this world. Like it or not, you have got to obey "THE WRITTEN WORD OF GOD."

I'm really blown away whenever I meet people who have been at the church all of their natural lives, that don't know what the bible have to say about the manner of which we should live. They have relied on the preachers to speak the word from the pulpits, but not really knowing if it is from the "WORD OF GOD" or not.

They have no devotion or prayer time in their own homes. They are determined that when they have given "God" some of their time on Sunday, the rest of the week is their's to live as they are pleased to do so. Truthfully, we are witnessing many people who have determined to turn the churches into the largest party the community has ever seen.

Too many of the leaders and the parishioners have either allowed or caused people to believe that there is nothing really going on at the church! Oppressed people are looking for an escape, they are not looking for deliverance and salvation. Many have been allowed to see the church as a cheaper party avenue. They can put a few dollars in the offering, if any at all, and dance like its broken!

Some churches had began to serve coffee and donuts or danishes, to be consumed in the sanctuary for a price, while the service is going on. Now I hear of other so called churches that are serving mixed drinks, and offering food entrées. All of these things are going on while the people purportedly claim to want to hear from "God."

Entertainment Up Front and Center

The people of the churches are so intermingled with the entertainment business of the world. It only makes since to the leaders of the more secular influences, to make as much money as possible, while they have the people's attention. The churches are no longer satisfied with selling dinners on Saturday. They have grown impatient with pew rallies and fundraising drives.

The business of the church is highly involvement from all of the people from the leadership all of the way down to the lay people. The motto now adapted in the churches is work smarter, not harder! It's easier to let people come to the cash register than it is to walk about the church and the community seeking those who are willing to donate to the cause of the church.

Somebodies about to get a whipping from the "Lord!" Many have disdained the written account of *"Jesus"* whipping the money changer out of the temple. They have turned the scripture to a meaning more beneficial to themselves.

Disdained God's Order

The bible says; *"they that preach the gospel should live of the gospel."* Meaning, that we as the preachers of "THE GOSPEL OF THE KINGDOM," that we should also be the first partakers of the teachings to which we deliver to the people.

The scripture has been reinterpreted to mean that preachers ought to make money as result of their message. Many entertainment schemes have been put into place, for the sake of keeping the people's attention, to keep them coming out to the church.

The so-called *Hip Hop Gospel* era, which is a lie straight from Satan, have infiltrated the churches. Churches that embrace that genre of music, have fired the musicians of the churches to hire musicians from the nightclubs who are more familiar to the secular influences of the music.

They know how to make the people want to get on up and dance! Only their music is powerless noise, void of the anointing to destroy yokes. Somehow the entertainers are convinced that "God" doesn't care anymore about the music and the purpose of the churches. Entertainers know how to get the crowd all stirred up and emotional.

They have turned their craft onto the churches, whereas the people are expressing the same tearful emotions that are seen at the concert. When talking to them, many are adamant that "God" have blessed them to make money with their gifts of music. So they play for the churches on Sunday morning, and play for the people of the clubs on Sunday evening.

There is no conviction of the spirit in their hearts. They have long since shunned holiness and righteousness. They could really careless who get saved and delivered. They will hand those same people a business card telling them where to find them at the club. Many of the people of the churches have witnessed the musicians play like wild men, and then walk out of the sanctuary as soon as the preaching begins.

Many of the praise teams now look like the on stage performers on the television. As a young boy growing up in the churches and even in our home, I was always taught the men don't wear hats in the house or inside of the building. Now the musicians are sitting on the instruments in the services wearing hats. The women are wearing jeans with the holes in them all of the way up to their thighs.

Absolutely, no uniformity among the singers and the musicians. The choirs used to wear robes, while the praise team members all wore a uniform sanctified for the service. People knew the differences when they entered the sanctuary. Now many churches have allowed secular entertainers to grace their pulpits to speak to the people. "God's" not pleased!

Because they have disdained the order of "God," they say that they want messengers who keep it real! Those who are truly "ANOINTED OF "GOD", are set to the side for the more entertaining persons, who know how to move the crowd. They say that the preaching of the gospel is old and outdated. People want to hear something different, they are tired of the same old messages.

I have seen people flock to churches where the preachers are using profanity and talking sexually over the pulpits. These types of messages are hyped with great applause and most likely never a complaint from the audience. I have spoken with a few cussing preachers who are convinced that "JESUS" must have used some profanity, because of the Pharisees and Sadducees.

They're Not Going to Do It Like Jesus

Satan have deceived many of the leaders of today, They have been led to believe that they can do things much better than "JESUS CHRIST" did things back in the days of the scripture. Perhaps they might even believe that there is just no way that "JESUS" could know about the people of today, as people are not even the same as they were back them.

Disdained God's Order

There is not a spirit that *"Jesus"* does not see it or know of its origin. There is nothing that the "Lord" can't handle. Regardless to what you may have chosen to believe, *"Jesus Christ"* is in total control. He need for us many times, to get out of the way and to remove ourselves as authoritative figures so that He can move in and deliver the people from themselves and from the power of Satan.

Those of whom are acquainted with *"the spirit of God"* and the movement of the spirit in the churches, are often sitting by the sides of the ministries watching the people blunder and dishonor "God." No matter of whoever you are, the other people of the leadership are not going to receive you. They are adamant that they are not going to do things the same way that *"Jesus"* did them.

How ignorant and stupid it is for someone who says that they are *"anointed of God"* to lead the people of the church, to disdain the one who can change things at an instance! He have the final say, even though He may not have spoken to you as of yet. You think about it for a moment, you don't even talk to people anymore once you have realized that they are not following you.

You need to ask yourselves; *"is "God" wasting time with me?"* Are you just a waste of "God's" space and intention for you to lead the people? Many of the churches used to sing a song which went on to say; *"What Do You Want The "Lord" To Say?"* What should the "Lord" say to you? If and when He speak to you, what are you going to do as result?

Is "God" really going to say; *"well done my good and faithful servant, enter into the joys of the Lord?"* Too many do not follow the *"word of God,"* if so they would remember when *"King Saul"* disobeyed "God." "God" rent the *"Kingdom"* from him, and He would have nothing ever to say to *"Saul"* again.

Blatant disobedience and outright defiance to the "Lord's"

instructions for you to follow, will get you into eternal damnation. "God" will fire you and remove you from leading the people. "*King Saul*" blamed his own defiance on the people's desires to worship and give reverence with burnt offerings.

"*Saul*" allowed for the people to touch that to which "God" had already forbade for him to touch. That which he was supposed to be leaving behind, he brought with him to report to the "*Prophet Samuel*," to suggest that he had indeed obeyed the "*word of the Lord*." Little did "*Saul*" know that the souvenir to which he brought back, that it would also be the convicting evidence which led to him being rejected by "God."

What purpose is it for "God," to give you instructions that you are never intending to follow? The people can cause you to end up in hell! One of the very most detrimental things that any leader can do is to try to tell "God," that you heard what He said! But, the people were just too precious to push them aside, just to obey His instructions. "*WOW!!!*"

Too Busy Trying To Tell God

Leadership in the "*Kingdom of God*," was never intended to be an easy task! Many people are difficult and unreasonable to deal with. However, "God" does not excuse us as leaders to forgo his instructions for leading the people to Him!

The "*Prophet Samuel*," undoubtedly developed a love for the King. As he lay in sackcloth and ashes, praying for "*Saul*." "God's" decision to remove and to reject "*Saul*" from being the King had already been made. "God" told "*Samuel*" to get up from praying for "*Saul*," because He had already rejected him and removed him from the leadership as King.

Many times we can see that the "*glory of God*" have departed the leadership of certain leaders. Amazingly those are the times that people want to intercede for them. By the time it has been allowed for the people to see and to recog-

Disdained God's Order

nize that the spirit of the "Lord" has removed, it's about too late.

Some will go on for years when allowed to do so, trying to convince "God" why those certain persons ought to be given another chance to continue on, as if to know more about the person than "God." I personally have had the experience of trying to pray for some certain individuals only to hear the "Lord" say to me, **NO PRAYER!**

Upon the spirit saying those words to me, the anointing left me like a garment that had been in the dryer for an extended period of time. I had no more spirit left in me to pray for those persons. I've been blessed in my life and my ministry to pray for different individuals in which "God" raised them from even their death beds. When the spirit said to not to pray, I knew to accept that "God," was not going to move on the behalf of those people.

We are often asking for people to do in a crisis, what they have never ever done in their lives, which is to have faith in "God." You need to know that "God" is aware of those who have denied the faith long before they ever had a crisis. Often we are asking for them to reach into the storage of the hearts and touch faith which has never even been allow to be there.

You can't be mad at "God" because He knows those who have never wanted Him. He's aware of those who only want what He can do for them. Should He speak to them, they would block their own ears, refusing to hear what the spirit have to say to them.

Ignorantly unaware, never being led of the spirit, people are praying for those in nursing homes and confined to sickbeds and wheelchairs, not aware that "God" have sentenced them there to die there. You do know that "God" can indeed be the "God" that he is, even whenever you may not understand His decisions.

The Sovereignty of God's Silence

I have seen some people lose their minds and will themselves to death as result of never accepting "God's" decisions. You see, if we don't want to see our loved ones and our friends lose their lives and their souls, we have got to get involved! To not only pray for them, but to speak to them telling them the "TRUTH OF "GOD'S" WORD," and show them "HIS LOVE" for them.

All souls belong to "God," but the soul that continues to sin, it shall die. NO EXCEPTION TO THE RULE! All must come to repentance, asking for the "Lord" to save and to deliver them from the life that displeases Him. The scripture tell us of the day to which we are now living, that men would be lovers of pleasure more than lovers of "God."

We are in the very days of which people will not endure sound doctrine. It is rather twisted to want to hear from the "Lord," but not until you have told Him what to say to you! You will never be given the power to tell "God" what you want to hear, and that he can only tell you those things.

"God" does not forget, neither is He slow to remember what He has already said to us in "HIS WORD." All will find out that "God" was never really silent. His words are spirit and they are life. The spirit never dies and the life is eternal. It is expected of all of us to hear what has been spoken, written, and settled in Heaven forever.

Based on what many of the leaders have had to say to the people of the churches, they have annihilated the possibilities for relationships with "God!" They have landed the people in religion, grounded and destined for eternal damnation. They keep on trying to tell "God" how they see that things ought to be in the churches.

"God" is a great counselor, and a great consolation. There is the better chance that "God" has been merciful to you, allowing you the opportunity to come to Him for correction and for healing of your mind. "God" called you because He believed in you from the beginning of your existence. He has also believed in your successful end as an anointed leader of the churches of "God."

You have no reason at all to fail "God" and loose it all in the lake of fire, in the end!

Chapter 8

He Has Already Spoken

For quite some time now, God has been perceived to have been silent. As certain situations transpire, and major events occur across the country, and the world, many people are questioning; "*WHAT IS GOD SAYING ABOUT IT?*" As good as God has been, there have been more critical reviews levied against Him, more than praising and worshiping Him.

People don't seem to realize that God is posing the same question to all of us. He's asking; "*WHAT ARE YOU SAYING ABOUT IT?*" Make no mistake about it, God knows whatever you have or haven't done either for Him or because He required it of you. God is not just sitting on the throne in Heaven waiting for people to pray, He seeks people to worship Him. He is not bored, looking for something to do, or seeking someone to talk to.

God sees everything at the very same time, and He sees everybody no matter where you are. Rather you knew or not, God could really levy critical reviews concerning you and me! But, He would be right about everything that He have noticed about us. The bible teaches us that God is love, and it also informs us that love believeth all things.

God already knows your worth and the value that you bring to the Kingdom of God. We are only here on the face of the earth because God believes in us. Just because you have been taught that God is looking for someone with good enough qualities and integrity, that doesn't erase the truth of the scripture.

It is rather frightening and disturbing at best to hear people pose questions, as if to bring God into accountability! It is total madness and chaotic to witness people expressing their disappointment with God. What about God's disappointment with you? What about the times you were called upon for the sake of the Kingdom of God, but you failed drastically?

You're here all because of God's plans for your life in the earth, and even better yet, in the Kingdom of God. We were made for the glory of God. Knowing this fact, many still prefer to behave themselves in ways which bring shame rather than to bring glory to the name of the Lord. Deceptively, most are led to believe that they only shame themselves.

Because we're made for the eminent purpose of the Kingdom of God, we are always on surveillance in the scope of the enemy's guns pointed at us. There is a perpetual target centered right on us. Our own personal misbehavior strikes the bullseye right smack in the center of the target! Only this target bears the name of our Lord and our savior. We simply are not our own, even though we might have chosen to do our own thing.

Comprehending the meaningful relevance of the plan of God for our own lives, requires much in-depth teaching and instruction for the task to be carried out. Even for those of us who know and are sure of the purpose and the direction to which leads the way to our destiny. It is yet very important to seek the counsel and the wisdom of the Lord.

One of the greater revelations that will be given to us, will be the realization of the fact that God had already spoken to our destinies completion to the very end. We are no such thing as a fluke experimental test, or some type of a trial version of the possible prototype for the Kingdom, to see if we can truly be what God wants us to be.

You may continue to believe that you are just a possibility, a may be, or even a probability in the plan of God, if you prefer. I'm here to inform you of the fact that God started His work on humanity from the end of our existence! He only backed up to the start at the beginning for the sake of the forward progression of time in the earth. I'm sure that most of us could never even fathom having been born fully grown and gray headed?

Of course that is where we see ourselves as we grow older and mature as the generational elders among our peers. We see ourselves getting closer to the finish of our existence here on the earth. From this point onward, whenever you see children being born to the earth, try to not only to view their arrivals, as their beginnings. Know from now on that they are only here because God had already finished the course of their true destiny!

While attending funeral services, it might help a bit to understand that the persons being laid to rest are the very same persons who came to us at their birth. Whatever their age, they were finished already before they ever got started. We often get lost on the tragedies and the illnesses which caused their demise. So much more of who they indeed were and their unique purpose is often overlooked, and or missed!

Through the churches many people are allowed to diminish spiritually, while they simultaneously grow into human globs, misfit for the Kingdom of God. The attitudes of the people in many of the churches nowadays is that of saying, you have been knowing that I am this way all along, why do you want me to change now?

These same people are coming before the churches seeking the help of the Lord, as long as they can remain who they have always been! The leaders who always allowed for them to to be who they were, have grown, and some have even

The Sovereignty of God's Silence

repented. The have recognized a long time ago, as to why it was that those persons could never get a break through from the Lord.

Many wrestle in the spirit of their minds as it relates to prayer. Even more-so than just praying, they tug at the thought of whether or not they can handle the Lord's response to whatever they are asking. This is the reason that they, so many of them are coming to the leadership of the churches and to prayer warriors to be prayed for.

I have been before many different people who were very adamant that my prayers were better than theirs, so they wanted me to go ahead and pray. Truthfully, I was able to since the reluctance to pray simply because they were not in right standings with God. It is very important that we who are in proper fellowship with God, to not only line up with God through the word, but then stay in line with God!

But let's be honest now, people know that they have not been living lives which please the Lord. Even sinners who have never read the bible, they know to be cautious when coming before the face of God to try to demand a blessing from the Lord.

So many people are consistently praying and asking God for things that are scripturally forbidden to ask for. I have found that many people want what they could never have! People are consistently asking for God to perform illegal acts in response, to their own iniquitous prayerful desires. Many sinners would love to be able to accuse God of sinning!

The detriment to this type of behavior, is that people are willing to ignore and to disobey the word of God, for the sake of satisfying themselves. The plight manifesting more clearly before us, relative to God being silent to the desire for people to hear from the Lord, is the iniquitous wicked hearts of people.

Iniquity ~ is the ultimate regard for sin in your heart. You know that you like it! Sin momentarily satisfies your craving, even though some of you will find yourselves down on your knees pleading before the Lord, asking that He would forgive you for doing what you know that you enjoyed doing.

You know that it was wrong and displeasing to the Lord, but your own heartfelt determination was to do what you desired anyway. Iniquity thrives in the heart of man, like as the seeds planted in the earth down in the dirt grow up to produce the products of the seeds! A good gardener knows that you don't just ignore the weeds, as they will also grow to corrupt the intended product of the seeds planted

For many years in the churches, I'd hear many messages that mentioned iniquity, but they never gave definition for the meaning. Iniquity was always tied together with sin. You really can't have iniquity without the sin. Sin will always be sin! Now we are aware that the regard for sin in the heart festers to produce iniquity.

As Adam sinned in the garden of Eden, he was also selling us out to the sin nature of the flesh forever. David said; *"in sin did my mother conceive me; I was shapen in iniquity."* All we had to do to be in sin was to be born to the earth. As we grew matriculating in the earth touching sin and sinful things we eventually developed a liking for it. If we would all just be honest, we would have to admit that we sinned, and we liked it!

Sin only have the power to become iniquity whenever you accept it in your heart as a child of God. We have the word of God and the power of the Holy Ghost to keep us from the power of sin. even though we are aware of this fact, we want to do what is indeed sinful anyway. That's iniquity!

Lucifer was already in Heaven with the Father, he made the statement; *"I will!"* Pride set up in the heart of this arc angel of the Lord. It takes a lot of pride to continue in iniquity. Those who choose to continue in their own way of choice, often become so hard hearted, not much grace is awarded towards them. Such hard headed-ness is the recipe for straight rebellion!

Stubbornness and pride mirror each other, as of which almost one is never seen without seeing the reflection of the other. The spirit of rebellion is seen on many different levels. Many criminal offenders are resting in prison as result of having been rebellious and stubborn in pride, outright refusing to observe and or to even obey the laws of the land.

Many leaders of our society, are stained with guilt riddled reputations, as result of dishonoring the truth and integrity. We see their willingness to altar the scriptural mandates for living, for the sake of their own popularity and financial wealth. They willfully live in iniquity from day to day, without any remorse or shame for disregarding the written word of God.

Likewise Lucifer also knew the truth, but truth got in the way of his pride. He insanely agreed to the penalty for his wayward action in Heaven. He knew that God would not stand for sin and iniquity in His presence. Pride blinded Lucifer, giving him the false courage to go ahead to fulfill the lust of his own heart. He wanted something that he can never have but it didn't seem to matter. Now that's crazy pride at best!

Drug dealers risk their lives and their freedom, on a daily basis just to have what they desire! They're standing on the street corners, and sitting behind the desk of many major corporations. They have succeeded to amass financial statuses, strong enough to allow for them to be the owners and the C.E.O.'s of the same corporations which employ many of the people of our communities.

Most of them who want it all, go out of their way to get it all, at any cost. As we have witnessed most of them, they often succeed, just to lose it all in the end. They have to give it all back just as if they never had it to begin with! They are aware of the fact that they just may lose it all in the latter end, but they refuse to let themselves focus on that fact. Pride increases to an outlandish rage, whereas many cannot even allow for themselves to care for their own souls.

The bible sternly admonishes us against abomination and iniquity! But people being led by selfishness and pride, they are diving in head and heart first, disregarding the warning of the scripture. We have never seen this behavior to the magnitude of which we are seeing it in these last days. Verbally and vocally people are telling the church to shut up, and to allow for them to live as they please.

Many of the television shows and the movies are making mockery of the word of God as it relates to living in sin. The actors go out of their way to acknowledge that they are aware of the fact that the references being made are from the bible. In the same breath, they also state that they don't want to hear, or to be judged by the bible, or from people of the church!

We see and hear of this contention from those who are of the order of the Mark of the Beast! In an effort to know what is the mark of the beast, it is of the most importance to be informed of what it is not! For several decades now, as far back as to the 70's I can remember many televangelist and pastors go forth to teach on the subject of the mark of the beast.

Most of them taught from a mechanical perspective, meaning machines and computers; computer chips; and or electronic attachments to the flesh. As scare tactics they taught this to get people to fear the future of the churches position in the society. We often wonder about the disrespect for the churches nowadays, much of it was bred through erroneous teachings relative to the coming mark of the beast.

A mark is a physical trait or even a scar, if you prefer, on the skin surface of the body of an individual. The bible talks about the mark being in the hand or on the foreheads of the individual's bearing the mark!

The detriment of this truth, is that because many are truthfully unaware of just what the mark of the Beast is, or even what it is all about. They are equally unaware of the fact that the mark of the beast is already here!

What is a beast, other than that which is become something dislike unto that of which God has already created from the beginning. A beast is that which is unrecognizable to that of which was originally created.

The scripture tells us to be transformed(*changed, relative to the spiritual reformation of ourselves through the written word of God*) by the renewing of our minds. ROMANS 12:2;

The bible never instructs us to go and have a physician to operate on our bodies, altering our appearance, changing our original gender, to look like what we were never created to be. God wants for us to never be conformed to the world, which is to do things only in ways that are appealing as well as pleasing to the world.

We can't be in total agreement to the Kingdom of God, and be simultaneously in step in total congruence with the trending behavioral systems of the world. God knew that it would be extremely necessary for us to be changed as result of haven been in sin. Our change must be pleasing to the Lord!

The only aid of self through this process of change would be for the sake of recognizing that we ourselves needed for the Lord to change us. We, must seriously desire for the Lord to come into our lives to change us from the relationship with sin to the very loving relationship with God through our Lord Jesus Christ.

People have great tendency to focus on all of the wrong things, most of the time. Pride switches our focus from the evil of sin, to the pleasures if sin! Keeping the sinners from

He Has Already Spoken

truly focusing on the penalty and the wages of sin, which is eternal damnation; death! One of the greatest designs of sin is to never allow any sinner who had ever been in sin as a lifestyle of living, to get out of it! To walk away as clean as a whistle. The bible teaches us that sin leaves a mark!

Those of who have been truly saved and washed in the blood of the Lamb, who are too proud to acknowledge that they had been set free from the bondage of sin, are dangerously overtaken with pride. God hates pride!

You need to go back to the altar to be freed from the filth and the stench of pride. No ifs, ands or buts about it! Pride is preventing you from letting go of the sin of your past, and from turning completely into the direction of the Lord.

Proud sinners, who are determined to stay in sin, are the only ones who are unaware of the mark of the stain of sin that they bear. Everyone else, especially other sinners see the mark very clearly. This is the reason that so many people will be seen staring at you as a sinner. We see many sinners jump to their own defense, suggesting that no one can judge them but God!

Many have heard me make reference to the statement made by many active sinners in the churches. They say;*"I'm just as saved as you are!"* They really mean that you are just as much a sinner as they are themselves, although you have been saved and set free from the bondage, and from all of the power and the darkness of sin! Sin blocks out the light of Christ Jesus in the lives of all individuals who are consistently living bound to sin.

The past teachers and many of the leaders in the churches never implemented the fleshly perspective relative to the mark of the beast, meaning the human bodies of the people, both in and on the outside of the Kingdom of God. Most people from the past generations have wanted for the people of the churches to be put at ease in the matter of displeasing

God by living in sin.

Most of us have lived on to have computers, whether laptops or desktop PC's, only to realize that whenever those machines were scratched up and or marked up on the outside, they worked just fine and allowed for computer access to ports and to website addresses.

In truth let's get physical! The people who are truly marked and bear the identifiable physical traits, are those who are of the homosexual and lesbian communities. Even those who are abortionist, who have no children alive and living. The mark of the beast is on this wise.

The mark is on the hands, and on the foreheads! The mark on the hands is relative to those who have reached out to adjoin themselves in support to the gays. They have even tried the behavior, being intrigued and curious. Iniquitously, they chose to do it anyway, knowing that it was not the natural design for the sexes of all mankind.

You can never un-touch that to which you have purposefully and selfishly put your hands out to touch. No such thing as accidentally touching the forbidden thing. God would have known if Eve had touch the forbidden fruit of the tree of Knowledge accidentally! When you've touched the forbidden behavior of homosexuality and lesbianism, you intended to do so. You did it with conscious intentions! You were big enough and grown enough to do whatever you wanted to do!

The mark in the middle of the forehead, is indicative of those who have accepted the gay agenda as a way of living. They have turned the truth into a lie. They have turned the detestable into that of sociable equality. They have either been convinced, or they have convinced themselves that they are justified to live in same-sex relations as a married couple.

The bible clearly talks about one man and one woman being in covenant relationship to please the Lord in marriage. The mark of the beast is on open display right in the midst of us. Those that are indeed marked are also reprobate in the minds. They can never see the need for a change to please the Lord. There is no such thing as a saved, and sanctified; Holy Ghost filled homosexual or lesbian.

God have already spoken it, and it's the truth!

Concerning this topic of interest, God is not at all silent! It's just that He has already spoken! God intend for us all to follow and to obey the written mandate of the scripture. Contrary to what sinful people are wanting from the Lord, God is not in the business of saying again, what He has already said in the scripture.

God's word's are eternal! If God is going to say it a second time, be assured that we are going to be required to live twice upon the face of the earth! Read the bible, you sill see that God has never spoken anything, that He went back the second time to say it again. His word is just too powerful to be thrown around in the atmosphere, just to see who will catch on to the word.

Rather you'd like to admit or not, God dealt with the atrocious acts of the gay agenda all of the way back to the 19th chapter of Genesis. Desiring for the problem or the situations not to be the same, I'm so sorry that you have been deceived, they are exactly the same! Fire is coming your way for the second time!

If anyone should be chasing someone, it should be you chasing God for deliverance and forgiveness! Unless you might have forgotten, this is God's earth that we are walking around up and down in it! God is not sitting by consenting to the acts and the wicked behavior of people all over the earth. There is no excuse! You are required to live by the written word of the Lord!

You have targeted the younger people of the churches and of the society. They are now defensive of you being charged and questioned about your behavior that is outright defiant and detestable to the requirement of the scripture.

Perhaps you might think that it's brilliant to make the younger people your allies, you are only taking them to eternal damnation with you, to burn in the lake of fire for eternity.

To the younger people of the society; you knew that it was indeed wrong when you were targeted and sexually mishandled! Now that you have chosen that same behavior as a lifestyle, and as a sexual preference, why can't you see the wrong that is still right in the middle of the behavior? Who silenced your ability to hear and to know that God doesn't approve of the behavioral choices?

Now that you have crossed the uncrossable, you have entered into the already spoken judgment of God. Many have been sorry, but only it had been too late for them!

You will be sorry that you never allowed for yourselves to hear the voice of the Lord God crying out to you to repent, and to change your ways! This is no joke!

Only yourselves and God, know whether or not, if it's too late for you! If you're arguing and fighting to stay in the alternative lifestyle that you're living in indeed, the better chances are that for you, it's too late!

You will have your part in the lake, which burns with fire and brimstone. Where the beast and the false prophet are. You will be tormented day and night!

God wasn't at all silent, you only refused to hear Him speaking to you through His word.

CHAPTER 9

Right Where He Is

He's Where; There; Here...

Chances are that wherever it is that you have been looking for God has been un-surety. Perhaps the breath of the Lord brushed across your hair as you passed by Him? I don't know! It is definitely more obvious to you than it will ever be to me that you missed Him!

He; the Lord, is often missed as result of the curious desires to find Him anywhere else than in the bible, the written word of God, or at the church. As sweet as it is that many of us in the Kingdom of God, we want people to see Jesus Christ in us, more often than intended people are not seeing the reflected images of Christ Jesus that they are indeed looking for.

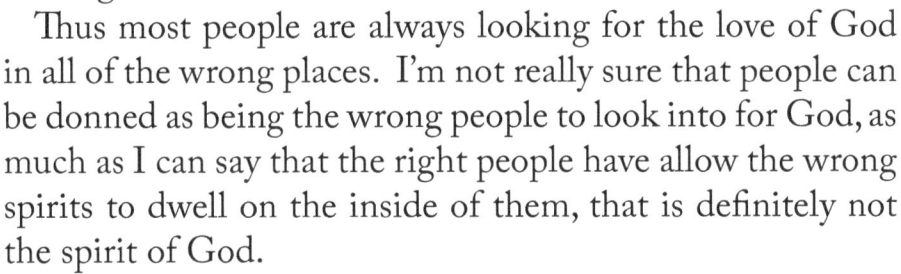

Thus most people are always looking for the love of God in all of the wrong places. I'm not really sure that people can be donned as being the wrong people to look into for God, as much as I can say that the right people have allow the wrong spirits to dwell on the inside of them, that is definitely not the spirit of God.

Like it or not, all people are God's, as He is the maker and the creator of all mankind. God said that; *"all souls are mine, the soul that sinneth(continues to live in sin), it shall die."* It's not very wise to declare that certain people don't belong to God. Those same people, as soon as they have been saved, set free, and delivered, they will also be privileged to worship God to the point of Knowing God, and God's purposeful agenda for worshipers.

Yes! People all over the face of the planet are suppose to see Christ living in us, alive and full of love. The vibrations of His presence are to be so felt that the realization of His being will cause even the most staunch doubters to know that He is! Any time that other people are in our company, they ought to since the presence of God in our company as well. Not many will allow for themselves to be properly informed and convinced of this powerful fact of truth!

Without any effort of our own, as the spirit of God speaks for Himself, the present power of God ought to command their attention. Because He is right here living inside of us right now, at the very core of our being, right in the presence of everyone that we come into contact with. Through us God is reaching out to touch the heart and the soul of all of the people present before us.

There is such a greater need for the people of God to just let Him be! Stop trying to create the reality of God for the sake of non-believers. He is God all by Himself! We need not to be so concerned about those who refuse to believe that He is! We who are the true worshipers of God, we need to know that we must worship God everywhere that we go and in the presence of everyone that we meet.

Whenever I say that we must worship God, I am not making reference to any type of Sunday morning activity. It is rather strange and quite different, the manner of which we behave during worship in the services, to the ungodly. Of course it is unacceptable for us to break out right in the middle of the street, or in the aisle of the grocery store, or on the work floor of the places of our employment.

Worship is so much more than just an activity or a behavior pattern of the people of the churches. Worship is a come on, not a put on! Worship is that which flows from deep within us. Worship require the inner core of our beings, not just the flapping of our arms, and the dancing of our bodies. Bodily exercise profits us little, as worship much more excellently, it profits us eternal rewards of life in Christ Jesus. So worship can be carried out anywhere that we are, simply because it is an inside flow of the spirit of the Lord, which may spill over to those on the outside around us.

Worship flows hot down on the inside of us to the likeness of lava down in the bottom of a volcano; *"for our God is a consuming fire." Hebrews 12:29;* The molten rock of the volcano is unstoppable and transforming to everything in its path. Things move and are incinerated as result of the temperature of the exaggerated excessive fire heating the rocks to the point that they melt and flow like liquid.

Worship acknowledges God with the ultimate appreciation for the fact that He is indeed God! Worship releases overwhelming love on the inside of us for God. Worship allows for us to know and to realize the extreme greatness of God. Worship causes us to know that the greatest power of our existence, flows through us entirely our bodies, souls, and our spirits.

Worship connects us to all the host of Heaven, allowing the angelic beings to know that we are Heaven bound human beings from the earth. Our worship gives the spirit platforms of satisfactory equality to the atmosphere of Heaven to work according to God's agenda for both heaven and earth. Worship lets the grace of God land among us while His mercy keeps us from destroying our chances of favor!

Many are not at all ashamed of worshiping God in the beauty of His holiness, they are too observant of non-worshipers, as if they really matter? God, is God; doesn't matter what anyone else thinks about it! Sometimes we pay too much attention to those who don't want God, careful as not

The Sovereignty of God's Silence

to offend them with our reverence for God!

I know that the greater reasoning for this behavior from the people of the Kingdom, is truly leveled beneath the greater need of understanding what worship is to God, and the benefit that it brings to us. It is past the time for the true worshipers to grow past the knowledge of what praising and worshiping God does, to the inner realm of knowing what praising and worshiping God truly is, in definition.

Knowing the definition of worship and the true meaning in what it brings to the throne of God, requires much profound research and study of the scripture. This is the kind of knowledge that no one acquires, without desiring to know beyond the surface. Wanting to please God more deeply than what may be experienced during a service, is the passion for which such experience of God can be realized.

Lucifer and his great ability to worship God, to the point that it moved all of Heaven, as he later displeased God in his own pride and iniquity, God replaced him with the greatness of humanity. We are so many more, as well as, so much more as worshipers to move the atmospheres of both Heaven and Earth. This being the one major reason that the masses of true worshipers are so divided, both in the natural and in the spiritual realm.

The now infamous enemy to humanity, knows more about worshiping the most high God, than most of us who have given ourselves wholly to worshiping God in spirit and in truth. The enemy being cast out of Heaven in the presence of God, is sent to be the prince of the air; he has left so much sinful residue spewed all over the earth's atmosphere polluting the way for worshiping.

We are not sent here only for having church services as saved people of the Kingdom of God, but as worshipers we are also sent to see the atmosphere of the earth washed and cleansed through worship and the word of God. Remember that Jesus Christ said to the disciples; *"and you shall be witnesses unto me both in, Jerusalem and in all Judea, and in Samaria, and unto all the uttermost part of the earth."* Acts 1:8B; See, herein is where we are to know of God's intention for the worshiper. We are living proof of the truth and the reality of God. Our true worship in the spirit and in truth, creates the witness that God recognizes as His own witnesses unto Him!

Take into account that God hear all of the noise of people who are suppose to be worshiping God in the churches. God knows the difference between what is just the noise of worship services, and true heartfelt worship. As we purpose ourselves to get into the spirit while worshiping, God is that spirit of which we are in need of getting into!

Know and be aware, that God knows whenever we have successfully arrived, and are seated in the heavenly places of the spirit. God receives true worshipers at all times of the day and of the night. It is always going to be yourselves and I, who are in question as to whether or not we have arrived into the presence of God for worship. And we are the ones who ought to know for sure that we have indeed made it to worship God in the spirit and in truth.

In the natural realm we understand the need for house keeping, and we show appreciation to the house keepers. All of the way up from the home to the largest corporate office buildings, house keeping is a must! So many people in the churches who desire to be the praise and worship leaders, they might take another look at the job if they were truly knowledgeable of what it is that they were actually getting into.

Just as we cannot force others to clean and to keep their houses clean, at best we can only express the need for cleanliness, and show them how to get it done. Likewise, leading praise and worship is so much more than an entertainer could ever even fathom. It is not at all about where, or into what form of activity worshipers are led into during a service.

It must be more extensively comprehended, that we are led to maintenance the earth's atmosphere, whereas we are the clean sweepers of the spiritual realm. We've got to come off of the surface while worshiping, and dive deeper into the belly of the realm of worship. So much is missed while worshiping in many of the services of the churches. As there is not enough teaching allowed which details the true meaning of worship; what worship really is, and of how to enter in.

However, housekeeping in the spirit realm is certainly more benefiting and rewarding. I want you to know that there are things done through worship and true praise, that even the angels are not awarded the privilege to do. Right here, right now, as worshipers, supernaturally we are given the privilege to step into the spirit realm right here from the existence of the reality of our natural beings, to do spiritual house keeping.

Now, it is imperative to know that such benefits of praise and of worship are not even available to those who are only involved with praise and worship from the perspective of their heads, only out of their mouths. Their hearts and the mouth never connect to worship God to make an impact to the spirit realm. These benefits are entered into through the portals of worship from our hearts!

From the city of our souls, at the very inner core of our beings, beginning at the control tower of the mind is where we intentionally worship and praise targeting the very heart of God. This is where we let ourselves into the depths of God's intentional purpose for us as the worshipers. It is bewildering to me how that so many are determined to worship God, outside of their own sober minds.

Unless you allow for your minds to sound the alarm to the recesses of your own hearts, worship cannot happen. As the minds must be employed to come along to the time of worship. The minds is the present examination room of the truth, and of all that it purported to be true.

Worship eradicates doubt and questions, as we can't both worship and question God simultaneously! Too many people are willing to allow for their minds to wander all over the place testing and examining forbidden data. Turn your heads over to the spirit, and allow your minds to be filtered and washed through the power of the written word of God.

Whenever you have reached the place where you can accept the written word of the bible as the truth of God, you will have then come to the point in fact to worship. Your minds when in doubt, is as a stopper removed from the drain at the bottom of the pool. It will allow for all of the substance of the truth to drain away to oblivion! Once the substance of truth has been drained from your minds and your spirit, there is no guarantee that you can ever get it again. It could be a permanent loss, forever!

Looking for God who has never been lost

Many are asking; "Where is God?" They say that they have been searching for Him for a very long time. Even many who have been saved and filled with the Holy Ghost, they are found at times questioning as to the where abouts of God. Most often, the simple but true explanations are too real, and to them they are too good to be true.

I am of the opinion that most people who say that they are looking for God, that they are not truly in search of Him. God has promised to those who search for him, to seek for Him with their whole heart, and as a result He will be found of them! *Jeremiah 29:12;* Perhaps many people are only seeking purported supposedly, ideas of God. Which doesn't constitute the only true and wise God of their intended search.

God who is most desiring to have relationship and fellowship with all of mankind, why would He intentionally hide

The Sovereignty of God's Silence

Himself from us knowing that we most desperately need Him? These questions are posed only for the sake of offering excuses for their lives which indeed are without the presence of the Lord.

His arms are stretched wide open compelling people all over the world to come to Him. God never behaves Himself like as unto sinful man. Even as Jesus Christ came to the earth, formed and fashioned as a man, still He never behaved Himself like as unto that of sinful man. Though sin was all around Him, yet He knew no sin! He never made us, only to be hidden from us!

Jesus never allowed for sin to get into Him, and He never got into sin Himself! If sin had gotten into Him, He would have become the sinful savior, though needing to be the sinless savior! If He had gotten into sin, sin in and of itself would have been transformed! Sin would no longer possess the power to land all unrepented sinners into eternal damnation. God saves us through the shed blood of Jesus Christ, but sin will always be sin.

If sin had gotten into Jesus the man, it would have possibly alleviated His omnipotence, deleting His power to save us all from our sins. Some people truly do not want to be saved, at least they have convinced themselves that they don't want salvation. However these are the same people who desire to hear from God of whom they have adamantly rejected.

They spend their time criticizing the worship of the people of the Kingdom of God. Seems to me, that it should make since to them to keep away at all cost, from all of the people that worship God, and from the truthful reality of all that is indeed worship. They should never put their hands out to any articles of worship, whatever they might be.

As they go out of their ways to criticize worship, inadvertently they are ignorantly bothering to handle worship. Unintentionally, they add damnation to their own souls, as they

Right Where He Is

can never add life, as intentional worship adds to the life of all who worship in spirit and in truth.

You're looking for Him where? Perhaps He's over there? But most likely He's Here! It is not that you are looking for God, it's where you're looking that is the issue.

Let me encourage you to calm yourselves, and to stop lying to yourselves! God has never been lost! He is as He has always been available to all of mankind. You can actually continue to look wherever you choose to find Him, or you can come into the knowledge of the fact that God is right here, right now!

Let me appeal to you that have been saved, set free, and delivered from your lives of sin and of shame. God never saved you just to leave you! He comes into our lives to stay here! The beauty of being saved by Jesus Christ, is the fact that He owns us. His love claims us, allowing for us to be recognized as the children of the Lord, forever.

It is oxymoronic to claim to be seeking and searching for God; who is here right on the inside of us, living and alive. He is right here where He's always been since He saved us. Others can look on you and see that the Presence of God is alive and well, living on the inside of you.

Many people can be dubbed as being the wrong people to look for the love of God, flowing out of them as they have never been washed by the blood of Jesus Christ. They have never been delivered from the power of themselves, which hinders the reflection of the spirit of God. They have never surrender to the will of God, to be used of Him, whereas other people can see God working in them.

Early on in the churches we were taught that God wants to use us. So we were taught to live so that God could use us at anytime, anywhere, with any people. As we are to become worthy vessels of honor for God to choose us and to use us, we are also to be transformed by the renewing of our minds.

The Sovereignty of God's Silence

As our minds are changed we are also made aware of the fact that God is living inside of us, as close to us as the very mention of His own eternal name. He is not where, or there whenever we call Him, He is here right now! Remember David said to us in the book of Psalms; *"He's a very present help in the time of need."*

God who is always here, He never has to come from anywhere! Clean living and righteousness makes us available to the ever present help of the Lord. Houses and many buildings will burn to the ground in a fire while they are waiting on the fire department to respond to the call to come an to put out the fire.

God is there to even extinguish the initial spark to start the fire. The fire never has the chance to get started to cause the damage that it will indeed cause, should it be allowed to burn. God knows the detriment and the exact danger of sin and iniquity. He knows the necessity of being in place to answer those who call upon His name. See, if you don't want to get in trouble, you don't have to!

God is here right now, right where He's always been since the beginning of mankind, and even since before then. If you want Him, you can get Him and you can always have Him! God is the authority of his own permission to help you. He comes to your aid unrestricted! Call to Him, from the inside of yourselves, now that you have been saved and sanctified, and filled with the Holy Ghost. You will find that He is here, already able to give to your need and the care most necessary for you.

Now you can say, that you have come to the very end of your search. Just ask for what you need from the Lord, knowing that it is His help that you need! You won't be denied! He knows what it is that you have been needing, He's been waiting for you to come to Him. Call Him! Now!

Chapter 10

Jesus Christ's Silence

He was oppressed, and He was afflicted, yet He openeth not His mouth: he is brought as a lamb to the slaughter, and as a sheep before her shearers is dumb, so He openeth not His mouth.   *Isaiah 53: 7*

And the high priest arose, and said unto Him, Answerest thou nothing? What is it which these witness against thee? But Jesus held His peace, and the high priest answered and said unto Him, I adjure thee by the living God, that thou tell us whether thou be the Christ, the son of God.   *Matthew 26:62-63*

And when he was accused of the chief priest and the elders, He answered nothing. Then said Pilate unto Him, hearest thou not how many things they witness against thee? And he answered him to never a word; insomuch that the governor marveled greatly.   *Matthew 27:12-14*

People Still Hear What Jesus Said, But They Wont' accept Who He Is**

I have come to understand and to embrace the trending error of the churches of these latter generations. It has been the inability to release the power and the spirit of "GOD" in "JESUS CHRIST, THROUGH THE HOLY GHOST," to the societies, and communities. Whereas people can know who "GOD" is! God is Love!

People think that they know love by what love does or

what love feels like. However, too often, people don't really know what "*Love*" is, for truth. "*Jesus Christ; is God's*" initial act of love to the world. See "*God*" only did it simply because He is it! "*God*" gave of Himself, He gave who He is! He's the gift that keeps on giving!

Those who handle the *word of God* from the platforms of preaching and or teaching, instructing in a classroom, they used to be required to have had an experience with knowing "*God*" personally themselves, firstly! Before ever determining to share the *word of Christ* to the others of the masses, there needed to have been an acknowledgment of the spirit in the lives of those who were desiring the platforms.

So many are handling the written *word of "God"* from platforms and pulpits of many diverse organizations and religions. Nowadays, the people have a scripture base knowledge of the words on the pages in the bible, but they don't have a relationship with the "*Lord.*"

They are verbalizing either what "*Jesus*" said in the bible, or they are voicing what they think that He ought to have been saying to us of these latter generations. They are both adding to the written word and taking away from the relevant meaning in the scripture, to be easier for humanity to receive! What an error!

They have no since of recourse as they take the readers, and the students and hearers of their lessons for granted. The very same teachers and instructors who teach that you should read and know for yourselves, are the very same voices who are telling you, that you are not capable of acquiring knowledge from the written "*word of God*," on your own! It is reported by many that the bible is too difficult to understand?

The word of our "*Lord,*" is not at all to be acquired through the aid of reading skills and comprehension. It is to be received through the spirit by faith and trust in the "*Lord,*" our "*God.*" You will never be successful acquiring the revelation

Jesus Christ's Silence

in the word of God, doubting and questioning, while simultaneously thinking that you are in the faith of God. Their determination is to place doubt in your minds even before you ever open the pages of the bible to read it.

They do want you to read the bible if you prefer to do so, they just don't want you to believe what you have read! They'd like to show you just how illiterate you just might be to accept such written data as the truth. The secular influence is suggesting that faithful acceptance to the written word of God, as for weaker people who need something to believe in. They say that; "*I believe in myself.*"

There is not enough space on the throne of your own heart for two to reign as Lord and King. You that choose to believe in yourselves, at best you are only standing and possibly reigning in your own way! The throne of your heart is designed for the presence of the Lord, Jesus Christ! God is a jealous God! He will have no other God before Him, and that includes you!

Many people in general of the earth's populous; including an alarming percentage of Theological scholars and even the unbelieving members of the society. They often debate and even argue against the validated relevance and the authenticity of what Jesus said and it's contextual placement in the written accounts of the scripture.

Some will take a chance on refusing to believe what Jesus Christ; our Lord and Savior, said to us in the written word. They are thinking that they can successfully question His state of mind, or even a particular feeling or an emotion that might have taken Him at the time of which He was speaking.

My reference is to the leaders and the so called scholars who study but question the bible. Such people never see any danger or the harm in second guessing the word of our Lord. I know that many of them think that they just are not ready to accept Jesus Christ as the Lord and Savior of their own lives, but they are missing the darkened position that they are putting themselves in.

More now than ever, such people are receiving support, and they are given consent from the higher ups of the churches and society, to deliver their own substance drained messages to the people. In my own opinion, this is the reason that people are no longer bringing their own bibles to church with them, whenever they do come to church.

They never even allow for themselves to feel convicted or guilty for shifting the thought processes of the people who once might have believed! They are convinced that they are going all of the way to their graves, haven shaken and stirred the mental and psychological strengths of those who might have been strong enough to believe the written word of God!

Going forward, I must inform you, that those people have deceived themselves to believe and to think that they might have won against Christ Jesus! God Never Loses!

Many nowadays, speak outright against what Jesus, Himself' had spoken to us! I have personally listened to debates over the scriptural mandates for Christian living, after we have departed the sanctuaries of the churches. As was spoken and taught to us by the apostles.

The passages and the statements often debated, are weighed against one another, as if to establish whether or not the words of Jesus' should be received as *"the authoritative doctrines of the powerful word of Christ."* Or as passive verbalizations; just as if spoken by a mere human being?

People go all of the way out to prove or even at times to disprove the meaning in the spoken words of Jesus' mouth. The debate is often to dissuade and to diffuse the faithful acceptance of the bible, and to strip the powerful piercing authority of the scripture!

Certain people of the churches of whom may be found to be readily agreeable and acceptable to relegate their negative discussions, are carefully avoided. They will speak to anyone that will listen to what they have to say. You don't even have to be a regular church attendee or a faithful tither to know of the attitude and the temperamental spirit of those who reject the scripture as being the word of God. We know this to be true!

It is most reasonable to know that the enemies of the bible would careless if you were not a true believer or even a faithful tither to the church. They might even hope that you had not heard the powerful truth of the bible. God's words are so powerful and alive, that it has an effect on anyone who reads and accepts it as the truth of God, that it is!

Make no mistake about it, Jesus' words are powerful to this very day, since from the day that He spoke them, at first. My friend, Jesus Christ is an eternal being! His blood, His words, His spirit and everything that is associated to Him are likewise also eternal!

Allow for me to say to you that, His words are forever speaking. Continuously saying what has been said! Eternally bearing the authority of His deity, and God-Head.

One thing that we know for sure is that Jesus in no way was, is, or will ever be known and recognized as a wimp! We are familiar to the story of Jesus, how that He was in the temple turning over the money changers tables, and whipping them in the temple who were selling doves and other merchandise, supposedly for the sake of sacrificing to the Lord?

Jesus exemplified fiery indignation; though righteously! He declared that my house is a house of prayer, but you have made it a den of thieves! Those words are yet speaking out loud to the leadership of the churches, world wide. So we know and are sure that Jesus was never afraid to say what was necessary to be said to anyone anywhere!

To this very day we yet marvel and worship the Lord over the words that Jesus spoke to the wind and the waves of the sea in a raging storm. He said "peace be still" and the wind and the sea obeyed Him. The waves lost their tenacity and angry attitude! Immediately they settled down and came to rest in response to the spoken words of Jesus Christ!

We are yet also likewise amazed as Jesus and the Apostles were journeying and passed by a fig tree in full bloom. Jesus hungered! He reached in to the tree to take figs from the tree but found nothing but leaves! What He said to the tree in response to the failure to find fruit, is what intrigues us even so much the more!

As a result of there being no fruit on the tree, Jesus cursed the fig tree and said to the tree; *"FROM NOW ON, YOU WILL PRODUCE NOTHING ELSE ANYMORE"* the tree withered and died instantly. The roots down in the ground withered, further signifying that the tree had in fact died. Not only did the tree die, but nothing else would ever be able to give it nourishment to live and to be alive. The ground for which the tree had been planted and flourished in growth, heard and obeyed the word of the Lord.

We remember when Peter and others were on the water fishing, toiling all night long, but they caught nothing. As they were coming in approaching the bank of the shore they see Jesus at a prepared fire ready to cook fish. But they had caught no fish to cook!

Jesus, had a little conversation with them, and like even most people of today, they were sure that He must have been missing something about them, they were professional fishermen. They were probably even a bit tired. They failed to realize that Jesus knows everything, and He already knew that they had nothing in the boat to cook and to eat!

Peter said firstly; we've been out here all night long, we're the fishermen, we know how to fish, but while he was still talking the spirit of the Lord pricked his spirit and Peter said to Jesus; *"but at thy word Lord we will launch our nets on the other side of the boat."* The word of the Lord called the fish into the net, so much so that the nets began to break, the boat had begun to overfill to the point that the boat might even sink.

Whenever Jesus said things, or gave a command, there were immediate non-contradicting manifestations that followed. Jesus knows all else that He has to speak to that are attached to your situation to cause it to be whatever it is, in an effort to bring the thing spoken to into fruition. All that heard the words of Jesus knew that he was indeed King and commander, whether they approved of it or not. Those who heard Him were compelled to follow Him.

The religious leaders of that time were angered to the maximum simply because they had spent years in the synagogue teaching. In one session of teaching, Jesus had totally annihilated and erased the doctrines of man and the religious teachings.

No doubt about it, we know that Jesus had the power of speech in his mouth! We could go on and on stating what Jesus said, and going over what He did, for which those of us who are given to study the bible and to seek the Lord for definitive understanding would all be in agreement. However, those who never heard Him would still determine within themselves, to be convinced that He is silent!

Have you ever noticed that we never hear any elevated discussions in depth relative to the actual meaningful purpose of His Silence? Most people flee the subject quickly fearing the possible transference to them to shut their own mouths and to be silent? We are driven to get to the understanding as to why it was that Jesus never said a word in captivity?

But, Was He Really Silent?

Most rational faith thinkers have come to the conclusion that whatever Jesus has said to us is right, and that it should be upheld and respected as the word of life to follow as a believer in Christ.

Many of the dividing lines among the worshipful persuasions of every race and sociable status of people all over the world, are installed along the chosen lines of scripture to establish what had been desired to be the biblical base for separating this group from that group. And the emotional from the more calmer groups of people, and so on; as people are continuously arguing over what is going to be acceptable and easily adhered to from the very spoken words of Jesus.

We need not always to be the ones speaking and lending our own opinionated thoughts of the scripture, relative to what Jesus said, and what He might have meant when He said it! As we read the scripture even being the least educated and literary astute, we soon come to realize that Jesus meant just what He said and said just what He meant!

In the writing of the four gospel accounts of Jesus Christ; we have observed that Jesus spoke often in parables. While He spoke in a manner to cause others to think, He always knew who He was talking to! He's not the author of confusion but of peace; He never spoke to confuse any people, but rather it was more often to cause them to think and to understand!

Alike many people of today who think that they know everything that Jesus knows about them and everything else, Jesus Christ; being God in the flesh, He had to put mere man in their place often asking and answering question to which they did not even have the answers to. Jesus had a way of making man think in ways that they had never even thought of thinking before. They thought they knew!

As a result, they were always talking and driving the people who heard them, like a herd of cattle on the strength of their words in the synagogue and in the temple. The fact is that most of us need to search for and find the times necessary for us to silence our mouths, and to stop speaking even when we may know exactly what we are talking about!

Jesus; told stories, He never told lies! Although He spoke

in parables to the religious leaders and to the people along the way as He traveled from place to place, and even to the twelve apostles. He did so to settle the spirits and the raging emotions of the people. It is often the natural behavior of people to get excited and emotionally stirred, to take the wrong actions, having misinterpreted a word or an action, or even a statement made.

There were times when Jesus plainly expressed to the Jewish leaders that He didn't agree with their teachings and their understanding of the scriptures, in which He never held His peace!

Jesus; being the manifested word of the prophetic pre-visualized spoken utterance of the prophets was no coward! He came to the earth born of a virgin, but make no mistake about it and don't get it twisted, He was all man, 100%! It didn't matter to Jesus that the leaders in which He was addressing, that they had a lot of money!

He knew more about their riches than they did themselves! He even knew how they went about getting their money. Jesus was not just a speaking mouth, He was God in the flesh, therefore He knew everything that there was ever to know.

So, as Jesus talked to His own creation; it behooved Him to straighten us out when the wrong thing had been spoken and to prevent us from thinking and saying the wrong things in our future, so as to place us on the righted path.

Of the greater messages spoken to us of the scripture, if and when we are able to hear the word of God by the hearing of faith and of the spirit, we discovered that Jesus spoke loudest to the entire world through His own silence!

The leaders and the Governor were blown away and messed up that this man which had turned the world upside down through speaking to the people, that He would say nothing. He was silent while the people railed on Him, and said all manner of things falsely about Him! Jesus was indeed careful not to speak up to His accusers. Alike the fig tree, those men could have, and they might even have withered and died, right there in His presence, instantly. He never came to the earth as a warrior to kill men, but He came as the suffering savior to die for all humanity! To redeem all men, and to save our souls! Atonement was His purpose, never was it murder!

He had already spoken out loud, since the time that He had been on the earth. He taught in their synagogues and in the streets and the wilderness. It wasn't just because Judas had betrayed Him, they already knew who He was. The Jews sought to stone Him on at least three occasions, He walked right through the midst of them, and they never saw Him. Those types of things are not easily forgotten.

His fame and the record of His powerful ministry had gone out throughout the land. It wasn't necessary for Him to repeat Himself, as that would be our purpose in the earth. Jesus was already aware as to the reasons that He had been taken captive.

He was facing carnal minded, religious men whose minds were made up to crucify Him! Since He had come on the scene, things would never be the same as they had been before. They could not compete with the savior of the world who healed the sick, caused the lame to walk, the blind He restored their sight, and He even raised the dead!

He confounded the wise men of that time, and did many wonderful things that could never be written of recorded, as there were too many. He wasn't really silent, as much as He was saving space for mankind to speak the word of the gospel of Christ, to all of the world.

Jesus; would never be the one responsible for sending the wrong message in response to the lies and the rumors that were being levied upon Him, or even of us! It's past the time that we as people come to know and to accept who Jesus is! Knowing who Jesus is, causes us to remember that He's got all power in His hands. We really didn't want Jesus to turn defensive against mankind. He made us all, He knows that He could speak and watch us all fall in death all at once!

Whatever Jesus did, mostly, we try to emulate, as we walk this walk of faith. Yet, it is more than obvious that we as a whole have missed it too often, allowing our feelings and emotions to dictate to us to open our mouths to defend ourselves; though we never saw Jesus defend Himself.

Jesus knew that you would be watching His reactions even before you could ever see Him in captivity to be crucified! It is the will of God that we as children of the Lord, that we would be calculative rather than to be counter-active! See if you don't know who Jesus Christ is, you are not able to become aware of what He has released inside of you! You're dangerous to the Kingdom of darkness, but don't know it.

No matter what may come upon us from day to day, there is a remedy in the written word of God to cause us to take action, whereas we are still in control and able to be the examples of Christ that we are supposed to be in a crises.

Although I must confess, things do get to be a bit challenging and trying at times; the word of God always assures us that the Lord Jesus is still in control, only we need to remain submissive to the leading of the Lord.

"Conclusion"

Selectively Silent

SILENT ~ *SPEECHLESS, STILL, UNEXPRESSED, UNPRONOUNCED, UNSPOKEN...*

I encourage you to take into account of the fact that God is well aware that you will not even speak to yourselves, knowing that you need to bring your body unto subjection! Being that your daily confession is that you are in control of your self, nobody tells you what to do, or what to say. You are also readily on alert to remind others of the fact that you are grown! Your choices of worship are dangerously in question, as result of your selective stubbornness and rebellion!

You tell yourselves to ignore holiness and righteousness, as it appear to get into the paths of your own chosen will to disbelieve and to misbehave. You have the power in your own mouth, according to *"Proverbs 18:21;"* to command your own behavior to be integral, relative to the mandate of the scripture. You know how long it's been since you first started thinking about committing those acts of sin and iniquity.

As desperately, as you know that you are needing to hear the voice of God speaking to you, can it really be said that He has not said anything? The major theme of this book has been that many believe that He has been silent. God who is always on time, as He can never be late, because He is everywhere already, wherever He is being sought after. Perhaps you left the scene just ahead of hearing His voice, because you were too impatient to wait for Him?

Perhaps whenever you go to your knees to pray to Him, it

is you, yourselves who do all of the talking? God will never enter into a wrestling match with anyone to speak with them, even as He's not going to fight for your attention. You might want to consider the fact that as you are listening for a certain sound of God's voice, God is the sound! Just enter into listening for God, at all times, with your whole heart! Be very careful, so as not to cause God to selectively bypass communication with you!

So many people of the past few decades have been taught to question everything! Thinking themselves to have become informed, as to how it is that they are to go about dealing with being prepared when God will speak to them. They have actually become fools right before the face of God! I'll ask a few questions of you for the sake of the possible reasoning, as to why it may be, that He has not said anything to you.

Is it possible that God was simply unmoved by your outrageous ungodly behavior, but did turn away His face from you? Could it be that He never moved into your space when you chose to do your own thing? Perhaps you expected for God to be as shocked as you were when you realized how low down you had sank, since that you had given yourself over to such insidious ridiculous and detestable behavior?

Maybe it was that you thought that you would try to test God by disobeying the word of the scripture? To your surprise, it didn't knock God off of His throne! You may be part of a certain group of people who are determined to prove the word of God wrong? No matter what your group does, it doesn't bring God down to the earth to discuss the issues with you!

You have made God your target by vandalizing the property of many churches. Maybe you are a part of the radical groups that storms the parking lots of the churches, offering alternative offensive literature? You're determined to show

Conclusion

the people that attend the churches that the teachings of the scripture are all wrong? You want people to think for themselves, to decide that after all sinful living, according to the teachings in the churches, is acceptable for the human race. I am sure that you need to get over yourselves!

Are you really sure that He has not been saying anything, at all? You should know that if you really didn't want to hear whatever He has to say, the greater chances are that you just might not have even realized that it was His voice that you heard speaking? It could very well be that it was the content of the conversation, according to the written word of God, that you were never interested in hearing, that brought you to decide that God was not saying anything?

How much teaching have you had, that enabled you to know how to even respond whenever you hear the voice of the Lord speaking to you? How important is it to you to know the voice of God? Are you even aware that He doesn't speak like anyone else? He is not a man! Are you even willing to wait on the Lord to locate you?

Where are you? I mean, where are you spiritually? You go wherever it is that you choose to go to avoid coming into contact with the spirit of the Lord, on purpose. Sooner or later, those of you who are purposefully living out of bounds, find yourselves wanting to demand that God come where you are. But, all of the while, you adamantly have no intentions of ever leaving the foul putrefied spiritual atmosphere where you are living your lives right now.

There are really no words satisfactory for describing the period or of the span, or the occasion of God's silence, when as far as we know, He did not speak. People are adamantly convinced that God had never spoken to them, for them, or even on the behalf of them.

As we have studied the writing of the scripture, it has been discovered that there were actually 400 years of silence between the Old Testament and the New. From the book of "Genesis" all of the way through to the book of "Malachi", God had not only spoken, but had been speaking to the priest and to the prophets on a consistent basis.

God spoke to the people, on the behalf of the people since they needed the help of the Lord. And certainly because of the behavior of the people! They had gotten out of line with mandated righteousness of God.

It's been rather incomprehensible that God who spoke everything into to being from the beginning of creation, that He would refrain from saying anything at all for a period of time. By faith, we know that worlds were framed by the world of God. He said it and it all came to be into existence.

Those of us who are indeed the faithful children of God, our hope is built on the spoken, and the now written word of God! The very fame of God, if you allow me to say it like so, is all established in the earth on the power of everything that God ever said! The eternal fixation to all that God created by the word of His mouth, is what is responsible for all of the things that we are made knowledgeable of since the creation, being whatever He spoke from the beginning.

God's spoken words are so powerful that they are yet speaking out loud, even to this very day, since the very first utterance from His mouth to start the beginning. From an initial sound of utterance, to the forming of a completed syllable to speak a word. The power of God was accompanying the finished thought for a purposed establishment of words to create a sentence.

God has never spoken nor uttered a sound, only to apply the power of His deity afterwards. GOD'S POWER FOREVER PROCEEDS WHATEVER IT IS THAT HE SAYS OR WILL EVER SAY! This is the reason why the word of God says to us that *"before the world was, I Am!"* You see, God never framed this world by words alone, but by His spirit which accompanied the words which He spoke! The power of God's spirit is the compulsion that pushes His words, causing them to leap into manifested action!

You should remember the 4th chapter of Matthew; the spirit of the God; drove "Jesus Christ" into the wilderness to be tempted of the devil. Satan thought that he would challenge "Jesus Christ" to turn the stones to bread, seeing that He was hungry after fasting 40 day and nights. Jesus said to him, *"man can not live by bread alone, but by every word that proceeds out of the mouth of God!"*

"Jesus Christ"; being God in the flesh, manifested as an human being, to be with us in the earth. He knows even to this very day, that man cannot live by only what they eat naturally. They must also satisfy the hunger of their spiritual appetite, feasting upon the meat of word of God. Satan never asked, as he was never interested in the true spiritual diet for mankind in the earth, as it would never benefit him in any way.

Many people are confused, bewildered, and spiritually confounded because of what someone had spoken, and said that it was a word from God, that told them to say it. They never even stopped to examine the spoken word to see if the power of God even accompanies the mouth of the person speaking, or even the spoken words! People are very quick to believe what some person may have to say. They are very hesitant to seek the face of God to hear what He has to say to them!

No doubt about it, God never leaves space for anyone else to be who He is! He will also show up without a question that it is God; Himself! There just may be times whenever the prophetically spoken word to an individual, may even be too wonderful for the messenger who spoke the word, to conceive it! Therefore, God stamps the word with the approval of His own spirit!

People show up to community events, city counsel meetings, revivals, and many other public and political gatherings to hear certain selected panalyst and keynote speakers. They were never really interested in hearing what the speakers and the themes of the forum were all about. They only wanted to see the persons, intending to ignore their messages.

Most who attend the churches are not really interested in hearing what the spirit has to say to the churches. The ears of the common hearers nowadays are completely closed to sound doctrine. They are mostly interested in the musical entertainment of the choir and the praise teams. Messages and or sermons that are not accompanied with a tune, are a turn off to them.

It is rather comical, but also heart breaking to hear the younger generation say that sound doctrinal preaching is Old School and unacceptable! Every generation believes that they have observed that the world has been changed. They are determined to believe and to embrace that the needs of the people of the churches have also changed. It is however, that the people who attend the churches of today are not surrendered to the spirit of the Lord!

Back as for as to two decades, many people began matriculating to churches where the messages were lightened to allow for more user friendly atmospheres. The messages which states to the people of the world to come as you are, in my own opinion are totally in opposition to whatever the Lord meant! The one size fits all mentality has been severely abused and misconstrued as it relates to the churches.

It is dangerous to apply the ideas of science and of the worlds influence to the meanings of the messages in the churches, according to the written word of God. What God says is what God means! What the world means and whatever God means are totally opposing realities. The world can't tell you what God means in His own word!

You are aware of the stress and the frustration brought

upon you whenever someone else tries to tell you what you meant by what you said. While the other people of the world can't rattle or frustrate the spirit of the Lord, their mouths can cause the spirit of the Lord to be silent right there where all of you are, during the time of your discussions.

You need to be informed of the fact that God is always able! But, His ability, does cause Him to over ride His own righteousness and the establishment of His word. God is forever all powerful and full of Love for all of mankind. But don't get it twisted, His love doesn't ever cause God to soften the foundational platform on the truth and the power of His word, of which it is in Himself!

God stands in His word, while His word simultaneous stands erected and solidified in Him! Great beast and huge military equipment, and even airplanes can be tilted over and turned on its side! It is usually all about knowing the right angles to reach underneath to start the flip. Much skill is required to complete such an almost impossible task! The skillful abilities of man are mind-blowing, and often outright unbelievable.

But even if all of the world joined together with all of their diverse military strengths and knowledgeable skill, there will never be any tipping over, over throwing, or turning God on His side! God will turn the world, by the way of the earth, on its side! He is going to shake all of the sin out of it, in the end! It is only because of God's mercy that He has not already turned the world on its head. The heads of the countries have been corrupted for quite a while now!

While the people of the churches are trying to force the spirit of the Lord to say that its okay now for the people to live against the word of God in these latter generations, they need to get back to repentance, because God will never change! The arm of the Lord has been revealed to humanity indeed, but it will never be twisted! God will never say "uncle", nor will He ever surrender to the will of humanity! God has already spoken to the world, to humanity; through the written word of God.

God will never be found to be at fault that mere men of these later generations have determined that God perhaps should rethink the word, and say it again a bit softer for us. I repeat that God is not like man, He has already said what He meant out loud with very bold intentions. One of the things that many people have missed through the word is that, *"the way of the transgressor is hard!"*

That is the reason that it hurt so bad and it stings like crazy to realize the bursting of your bubbles. Just when you thought that you had the spirit of the Lord considering your thinking about His word! God allows for you to get all heated up behind your on idealistic understanding and thinking. Just enough for you to see that your ways are never enough to settle the issues or to fix the problems of your lives.

You can not save your own soul! I know that you may think that you are all of that and a bag of chips, the direction of your soul's eternal destination, is only left up to you, relative to you choosing "Jesus Christ" to be your Lord and Savior. You've peeped into the book of "Revelation", and have read and discovered that hell is not the final destination, after all.

So you have also been influenced to discount, disrespect, and even to disallow the reality of hell. You think that the bible is so contradictory, that hell just may not even be real. Many have even claimed to be okay with going to hell, they say anyway. How could you ever be okay with hell, when you say that you do not even believe in hell? You for certain don't know where hell is, but the Holy Ghost does know!

You should have finished reading all of "Revelation", you would have also discovered that hell and death, being the last enemies destroyed, they will both be cast into the lake of fire and brimstone! So just maybe you're right, you may not be in

Conclusion

hell for all of eternity, but you will be burning in the Lake of Fire for all of eternity! And that's for sure, according to the written word of God!

Now just why would God talk again to you, or to any of your kind of people, knowing that you have chosen hell and death as your final destination? He came to the earth to keep us all from going to hell, and to the Lake of Fire!

Most all people have always been taught to be blissfully excited about their wedding! But there is very little teaching to maintain the marital bliss throughout the remainder of the marriage. Many say that it doesn't matter what the bible says, if the marriage is not working out the way that they want it to, they are walking out of the marriage.

The people of the world have been working on changing the definitions of marriage for a long time now. At first, they started out with defining living together in the same house, while maintaining a sexual relationship, as a common law marriage. Now same-sex relationships are referred to as common unions. Now legislation have made it lawful for same-sex unions to enter into permanent commitments, they now refer to as marriages.

How do you go about to change what God says in His word, yet desiring to have Him to speak to you? So, now that we are adamant to speak a word of correction to the gay communities, let us not forget that all sin will result in the eternal Lake of Fire! There are also those people, both male and female, who have refused to marry anyone, but they are sexually active!

It doesn't matter that many heterosexuals despise homosexuals, when both are out of order to the word of God. How disgusted do you really think that you're going to be to look across the lake to see the other sinners that you despise, looking right back at you! They could have told you that all of you were on your way to eternal damnation and destruction.

The Sovereignty of God's Silence

I have said before, but I will say again that sex is not the only sin! Every sin, in every form and of every origin is all just as bad as the other. They are all guns, deadly weapons designed to kill, with silencers attached to them. They make plenty of noises, but they silence that voice of God!

Finally, ~ is He silent, or are you deaf? You're probably not at all deaf, just stubborn enough to refuse to hear. Is He not speaking to you at all, or are you determined not to listen to what God have to say to you about your lifestyle? Does God even care that you will not hear Him, or do you even care that God has an interest in you? P. S. He is not suffering at your refusal to hear, but you will suffer the loss of your soul.

God is sovereign, He doesn't even have to decide on you for any reason. God continues to hold His arms out to receive you, even though you wont reach back. His plan of salvation is yet in effect. Even though you are determined to stay a sinner for as long as you can get by with it. You know, you keep on drinking and smoking until a physician tells you that you have destroyed your body.

You keep on doing wrong until you have a criminal record, including an extended prison sentence attached to your place of living. You know, now you have gotten yourselves into a mess that you can't get yourselves out of! So now you're calling for the help of the Lord. Even though you only want His help, not His miraculous change for your lives!

God know us all from the inside, out! Never be fooled enough to think that you have any hidden secrets that God is not aware of. Everything that there is to know about you, God already knows. Even when He does choose to talk with you! He wants to hear from you, the price for His consultation has already been paid on the cross at Calvary.

"Jesus Christ", signed His own signature for your acceptance in His blood. "Can You Hear Him Now?"